Ueno Park

Benten Shrine

Meteorological Institute

Asakusa Amusement Park

ASAKUSA

Ushijima Shrine

Imperial Palace and Plaza

Mitsukoshi Dept. Store

HONJO

Army Clothing Depot

FUKAGAWA

Nihon Bashi

SUMIDA RIVER

rial Hotel

City Hall

Ginza

Ichimura (Kabuki) Theatre

Navy Club

Tokyo   Bay

TOKYO

September 1 to September 3, 1923

TWO

MINUTES TO NOON

NOEL F. BUSCH

SIMON AND SCHUSTER · NEW YORK · 1962

First Printing

LIBRARY OF CONGRESS CATALOG CARD NUMBER: 61–5832
MANUFACTURED IN THE UNITED STATES OF AMERICA
BY H. WOLFF BOOK MFG. CO., NEW YORK, N. Y.

CONTENTS

ILLUSTRATION
SECTION

TOKYO: the clock at the Meteorological Institute, with its hands stopped at the time of the first shock.

Point at which north-south needle jumped graph.

Tokyo Observation of the Destructive
Earthquake of Sept. 1, 1923.

Magnification=2. P ......commencement : 2h 58m 44s. (G.M.T.)

a......commencement of the principal portion.

(2)......After-shock at 3h 01m 49s. (G.M.T.) t......successive minute marks.

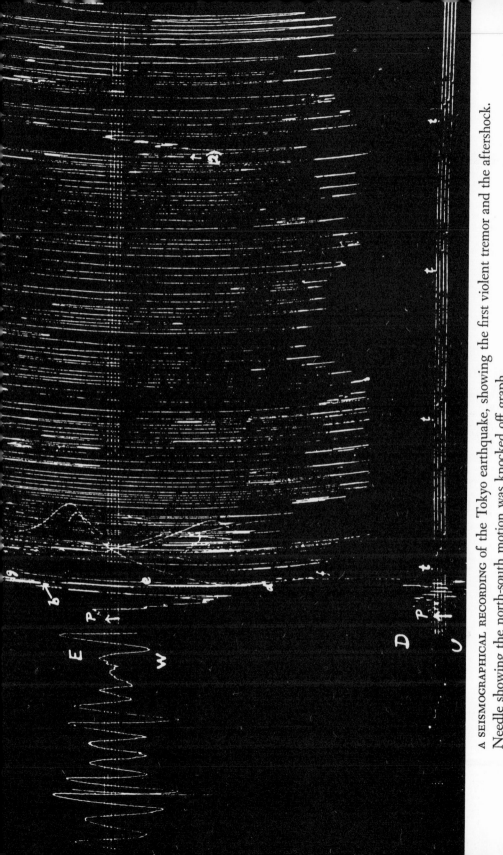

A SEISMOGRAPHICAL RECORDING of the Tokyo earthquake, showing the first violent tremor and the aftershock. Needle showing the north-south motion was knocked off graph.

TOKYO: the Yurakucho area, seen from the north side of the Imperial Hotel. The building in flames is where the Takarazuka Theater (known during the U.S. Occupation as the Ernie Pyle) now stands.

14

TOKYO: the former Army clothing depot, in the Honjo District, after the fire.

TOKYO: the Asakusa entertainment district, showing ruins of the twelve-story tower.

TOKYO: road outside the Imperial Palace, showing earthquake fissures.

18

YOKOHAMA: a street in the business district. Wheels on left are remains of a hand-cart.

TOKYO: soldiers and "vigilantes" standing guard against Koreans in the Akasaka District.

22

YOKOHAMA: burned corpses piled up in entrance to the Yokohama Specie Bank.

TOKYO: the Crown Prince (now Emperor Hirohito) rides out to survey the damage in Ueno Park.

CHAPTER I

NIHYAKU-TOKA

THE TWO HUNDRED AND TENTH DAY

O N THE LAST DAY of August, 1923, the world was wagging along in its usual hit-or-miss fashion but perhaps a bit more pleasantly than usual. In Germany, to be sure, the mark had fallen to a new low of ten million to the dollar; in Italy, the recently installed Premier Mussolini had ordered the bombardment of Corfu. Such troublesome developments, however, were in the minority, and those not directly concerned devoted their attention to much more festive doings. Barely a month after the death of President Warren Gamaliel Harding, United States newspapers gave much of their space to sport. At Saratoga, New York, Jack Dempsey, preparing for his championship bout with the Argentinian Luis Angel Firpo, sparred with an enormous Negro named George Godfrey. At Forest Hills, the National Lawn Tennis Association tournament neared a climax involving William T. ("Big Bill") Tilden and William M. ("Little Bill") Johnston, its most renowned competitors. Someone named Henry Sullivan—the first American to accomplish this later fashionable feat—had just swum across the English Channel.

The substantial notice which such athletic prowess was accorded by the press reflected, perhaps, the relaxed and confident state of mind in which the nations found themselves five years after what was then naïvely known as *the* World War. It was the start of a decade in which the records to be set in all forms of sport seemed symbolic of new peaks to be attained in many other fields. On the New York Stock Exchange—which was drawing a deep breath for its subsequent climb—the close was strong: General Motors 15½, U. S. Steel 93⅛, and New York Central 100¾. Late-afternoon crowds rushed to get out of town for the long Labor Day weekend. That evening, perhaps after dining at one of the new "speak-easies" that had started to make their appearance in the city, theatergoers had their choice of such items as *Little Miss Bluebeard*, starring Irene Bordoni, *The Green Goddess*, starring George Arliss, and Anne Nichols's *Abie's Irish Rose*, then in the second year of its unprecedented run.

As the playgoers came out for the first entr'acte in New York, it was already past midnight in London, where the *Times* had gone to press with the news that Cosgrave had won the Irish election and that H.R.H. the Prince of Wales was getting ready for his trip to Canada. The evening was just beginning in San Francisco, where the best movie in town was *The Hunchback of Notre Dame*, starring Lon Chaney. Out across the Pacific, the surf riders at Honolulu caught the last wave of the afternoon as the shadows —first of the palm trees and then of the abrupt hills behind them —lengthened across Waikiki Beach. Farther west, at the international date line, it was only early afternoon—though, of course, of the next day, September first. In Tokyo it was still a hot and muggy Saturday morning.

In Japan, the first of September, like a good many other days, has a traditional name and character. It is Nihyaku-toka, or Two Hundred and Tenth Day, counting by the old calendars by which the new year was considered to start at the beginning of February.

According to tradition, Nihyaku-toka was, as it still is, a day to be wary of—a day likely to bring a typhoon or something equally unpleasant. Perhaps some half-conscious recollection of its reputation was in the back of the mind of a young magistrate named Kunio Sumiyasu as he set off for the Yokohama District Court that morning—or perhaps it was just the humid weather. In any case, after starting out he thought it looked like rain and went back for an umbrella. When he got to his lodginghouse, he gave the matter more consideration and decided that he didn't feel enough like going to work to do it. Instead, he went back to sleep—thereby, as things turned out, saving his life. By noon, the District Court, Japan's first brick building, was a heap of rubble in which were entombed the forty-four occupants, including a dozen of Sumiyasu's judicial colleagues.

In 1923, weather bureaus had not yet acquired the whimsical convention, now so deeply relished, of calling typhoons by feminine first names, but the typhoons were otherwise much like those of the present. On this Two Hundred and Tenth Day there was, in fact, a typhoon churning around a hundred miles or so north of Tokyo, and it may well have been the influence of this nameless storm that had caused rains early in the morning and humidity later. In any case, by 11:30 the skies had cleared and a hot sun blazed down on Japan's capital and on the bustling port of Yokohama, seventeen miles to the south.

Many residents of both towns, like the townsfolk on the other side of the world, were planning to go away for the weekend and busied themselves accordingly. One of these in Tokyo was a twelve-year-old girl named Makiko Aoki, whose father made spectacle-frames in a small factory not far from the Sumida River and sold them in a shop nearby. Her mother was spending the summer at the seaside resort of Oiso, an hour and a half to the south of Tokyo on the coast of Sagami Bay. Makiko's plan was to have an early lunch and then go to Oiso on the afternoon train. She wrapped the overnight things she would need in a beach towel and put on special clothes for the excursion, which would doubtless be the last one of the season. These clothes included a new dress and, even more unusual, her first pair of laced shoes instead of ordinary clogs, or *geta*.

A mile or so away, in the same crowded section of town but a little farther south, stood a small private hospital clinic run by a widely respected physician named Dr. Eikichi Ikeguchi. Dr. Ikeguchi, a graduate of the Nippon Medical College, had, at the age of forty-two, built up an enviable practice in his neighborhood. Among his patients were that section's richest family, the Yasudas, who controlled the Yasuda *zaibatsu*, or industrial combine, fourth largest of Japan's big four. In the office of his clinic, Dr. Ikeguchi was attending to his last patient of the morning, a man with a jagged piece of glass embedded in his ankle.

THE SUMIDA RIVER is a brown and sluggish stream which winds through Tokyo more or less like the Thames—which is about the same size—through London. The Honjo district, along its lower reaches, where the doctor and Makiko Aoki lived, was one which had known better days. Before 1868, when Tokyo was still known as Edo—after the owners of its original fortress—and when the Shogun, rather than the Emperor, lived in the great castle which had replaced this modest stronghold, the area had been a desirable residential district. To understand what had happened in the interim involves a brief glance at the capital's remarkable history.

In 1590, when the renowned Tokugawa family first acquired title to Japan's hereditary Prime Ministership, Edo became the political capital, while the Emperor and his court were left to rusticate at Kyoto. To ensure the permanence of this arrangement, the family devised an ingenious method of enforcing the loyalty of Japan's major feudal lords, or daimyo. This was to insist that each of these daimyo—of whom there were about two hundred of varying wealth and influence—spend a major part of each year at Edo. When any one of them departed for his provincial stronghold, he was required to leave close relatives at the capital as hostages to guarantee his good behavior in his absence. In Edo, most of the daimyo settled on the high ground south or west of the palace. Their mansions, each surrounded by the dwellings of some two to twenty thousand retainers, servants, and tradespeople, formed a cluster of villages. As Edo developed from a provincial town into a major metropolis, these villages became its principal suburbs.

The armed retainers of the daimyo, numbering in all well over a million, were the famous samurai, those knightly warriors whose harsh creed of courage, loyalty, and fierce pride, known as *Bushido*, set the character pattern for the capital and thus for Japan as a whole. As the daimyo died off or their fortunes fell, leaderless samurai, known as *ronin*, were forced to give up soldiering for tamer careers in commerce or the professions. (A cardinal point in *Bushido* was contempt for all forms of mercenary gain—which is why even today the custom of tipping enjoys small favor in Japan.) Honjo, where a few of the major lords had their town houses along the riverbanks, was an area in which many former samurai had settled down; and it was here, indeed, that the tragic incident of the Forty-Seven Ronin had reached its gory climax one snowy January night in the winter of 1703. Celebrated thereafter as a classic demonstration of the samurai code, this affair concerned the retainers of a minor daimyo who provided a spectacular proof of their devoted loyalty. When their lord was obliged to commit ceremonial suicide in consequence of a quarrel with one of his peers, they took vengeance on the latter by cutting his head off—after which they all committed *hara-kiri*.

The house in which the beheading had taken place stood in the very block now graced by the Aoki spectacle-frame factory. By 1923, indeed, the whole area had been given over to small plants like Mr. Aoki's or to modest offices, warehouses, and middle- or lower-class residences. The most conspicuous architectural feature of the district was the wide, squat rotunda of the *sumo* stadium, some fifty yards in diameter, which vaguely suggested the potbellied shape of the wrestlers who contended so ceremoniously in the earthen ring. Almost the only reminders of the old days were the two Yasuda compounds, standing side by side along the left, or east, bank of the river, which were the Tokyo headquarters of both branches of the family. Yoshio Yasuda, head of the junior branch, had a mild case of t.b.; Dr. Ikeguchi cared for the household as a whole and called there daily.

Next to the Yasuda gardens, with their carefully landscaped ponds, where somber carp drowsed in the tepid water, and separated by these gardens from the river, lay a broad area of unused ground. This ground had been, until recently, the site of the Army Clothing Depot, where military uniforms were manufactured by local workers and then stored for shipment, by rail or sea, to various units scattered about the country. About a year before, the authorities had decided that the Depot was inadequate to handle the expanding needs of the armed forces and had moved the whole installation, including sheds and warehouses, to a more spacious site elsewhere. Soon the former Depot, an untidy wedge-shaped patch of some fifteen acres, was to be converted into a park containing a school, a post office, and a municipal office building. Meanwhile, it was used as a playground by the children of the neighborhood and by athletic groups representing the nearby Nippon University High School.

The decline of the district along the lower reaches of the Sumida —by this time comparable in character to the East End of London or the Greenpoint district of Brooklyn—was all a part of the astounding change that had taken place in the city as a whole during the previous seventy years. With the opening of Japan to foreign trade and influence in 1854, and with the restoration of the

Emperor to power more or less commensurate with his divine status
in 1868, an extraordinary metamorphosis had taken place in what
was then renamed Tokyo, or the Eastern Capital. In the space of a
few decades, the city had abandoned feudal rusticity for the loud,
dusty commotion of the twentieth century. The smart place to live
now was far inland from the swampy riverbanks, in the low hills
southwest of the palace, where the foreign embassies had been
built so as to be—like the earlier feudal mansions—close to the seat
of authority. Meanwhile, after an initial drop—when many
daimyo, no longer required to stay in the capital, had retired to
their country estates—Tokyo's population had risen to almost three
million, making the city the world's largest after New York and
London.

One of the most impressive signs of Tokyo's new importance as
a great modern metropolis was the number of foreign visitors who—
though living residents could still recall the days when no foreigner
dared set foot in Japan, let alone in its capital—now came there
every year. Before the World War, such visitors had been obliged to
stay either at Japanese inns, where they had to sleep on floor
mats and eat with chopsticks, or else at an overcrowded and rather
shabby European establishment grandiloquently called the Teikoku,
or Imperial, Hotel. What Tokyo needed, obviously, was a really
first-class replacement for this dingy hostelry—something along
the lines of Claridge's in London, the Ritz in Paris, or the Plaza
in New York. The war had delayed execution of the plan to
provide one, but immediately afterward work on a new Imperial
had begun in earnest. The architect was a youngish American
named Frank Lloyd Wright, who had been chosen through a
characteristically Japanese process by the delegation sent to New
York to find America's top man in the field.

The delegation had put up at the Plaza, whose location on
59th Street was especially convenient, since it made it so easy to
seek advice on the problem from the person best qualified to

provide it. This was Mr. Aisaku Hayashi, manager of the celebrated Yamanaka Gallery, which was only two blocks away, on 57th. When Mr. Hayashi said that he knew just the man for them—by a fortunate coincidence, indeed, he was one of the gallery's best customers—the members of the delegation knew at once that they need look no further.

Baron Kihachiro Okura, the chairman of the Imperial's board of directors, was a famous connoisseur whose interest in art was knowledgeably shared by Wright; the latter's taste for Japanese prints had been acquired in the course of a stay in Japan before the war. Kishichiro Okura, the Baron's debonair son, who headed the delegation, also hit it off with Wright immediately; his own aesthetic interests lay in Western music, but he felt, as he explained later, that Wright's unconventional union with a Mrs. Miriam Noel provided an interesting "variation" in the human concerto. No one in the delegation was too insistent about examining Wright's previous achievements in the luxury hotel field. This was perhaps just as well, for there were none to inspect.

When Wright arrived in Tokyo to start work, a few minor difficulties developed, but the fact that the new building bore little resemblance to any hotel—or, indeed, anything else—ever seen in New York, London, or Paris was not one of them. Baron Okura and his colleagues were products of a culture in which the disposition of fifteen old stones on a sandpile may convey meanings more profound than the Parthenon's. For them, the distinction between ordinary Western structures and Wright's concept of an improvement on them was thus conveniently blurred. What bothered them much more was Wright's apparent disdain both for the most elementary principles of engineering and for the budget. The latter had been set at three million yen, the equivalent of half that many American dollars, which had seemed quite enough to get along on. Wright, however, when too far into the job to leave the directorate the option of replacing him, had coolly demanded three million more; and finally, before the work was completed in the summer of 1923, the total cost had come close to nine. Happily for all concerned, Baron Okura was in a position to underwrite the deficit and disposed to do so as a gesture of international good will.

As to the engineering troubles, it was hard to say which was worse—Wright's scorn for the traditional means of forestalling possible damage by one of Tokyo's frequent earthquakes or his strange passion for electricity. In consequence of the latter, he had installed not merely an electric kitchen but even an electric system for heating the bath water, which—like some of his other notions—had proved lamentably unworkable. Whereas the humblest Japanese rural inn can provide all its guests with a boiling-hot bath at any time, and usually one big enough for them all to take together, Wright had insisted upon a separate bathtub for every room. He had then compounded this extravagance by installing a heating system so inadequate that if half the occupants were to draw baths at the same time, the other half would be obliged to use cold water or to wait.

The hot water problem could, of course, be solved readily enough by having servants fetch the requisite amount in pails, after heating it over fires, but the earthquake menace was more serious. Downtown Tokyo is essentially a bog, where the water table lies within eight feet or so of the surface. The accepted building procedure was to avoid puncturing the surface of the ground with basements or other underpinnings. Wright, on the contrary, had sunk concrete piles all over the site and balanced the building upon these.

Nor was this all. As to the floors, Wright had argued that if they were held up by the outside walls in the normal fashion, they would fall down in a quake in case these supporting walls gave way. He wanted them to be supported by pillars in the center and drew the apt analogy of a waiter carrying a tray on one hand. Finally, as to the walls themselves, instead of making these a yard thick all the

33

way up and reinforcing them by steel rods and corrugated iron, Wright had insisted on making them wedge-shaped—thinner at the top than at the bottom—and had topped them with a flimsy sort of copper roof. What would happen in case of a really severe earthquake like the ones which had done terrible damage in the nineties? Nothing to do but wait and see; the new manager, Tetsuzo Inumaru, would have to solve the problem as best he could when it arose.

Now, on the first of September, 1923, Inumaru had a very different sort of problem on his hands. This was a banquet lunch to celebrate the formal opening of the hotel, which was scheduled for twelve noon on that very day. Two hundred distinguished guests had been invited, including the American Ambassador, Cyrus Woods, who was unfortunately out of town for the weekend. Inumaru, though only thirty-five, was an experienced hotelier who had learned the business from the ground up, after graduating from college, by working his way around the world from a railroad hostel in Manchuria to New York's old Waldorf. He was not nervous about the banquet but he knew that something could always go wrong at the last minute. Shortly before noon he summoned his staff to his private office on the second floor for a last-minute briefing before going downstairs to greet his guests.

The gala luncheon at the new Imperial was only one of a number of important activities scheduled in Tokyo that morning. Most noteworthy of all these was a small gathering at the Suikosha, or Navy Club, where Admiral Count Gombei Yamamoto, who had just been designated by the Emperor as the new Prime Minister, was trying to form his Cabinet. Various candidates for the different ministries had been coming and going all morning, among them another well-known peer, Viscount Shimpei Goto, who was favored for a key post—either the Foreign or the Home Ministry. Kenzo Fukuma, a young reporter for the *Asahi Shimbun*, Tokyo's biggest daily, was one of the twenty-odd newspapermen who were covering this meeting. As noon approached he was sitting in the garden outside the club, thinking that it was about time the Admiral came out to tell them what, if anything, had happened. He hoped that it would be something sensational that would enable him for once to get in on a story that was really big.

While Fukuma waited outside the Navy Club, another humbler member of the *Asahi* staff, a truck driver named Tatsuo Shiraishi, was dozing on a train as it drew into the platform at the resort of Nebukawa, beyond Oiso on the rim of Sagami Bay. With eight of his fellow drivers, Tatsuo was off on a long-planned holiday excursion to the larger resort of Ito, which was noted less for its beach sports than for even livelier pleasures, of a sort similar to those available in Tokyo's Yoshiwara, or licensed red-light, quarter.

Northeast of Nebukawa, the wide crescent of Sagami Bay curved past other resorts and fishing villages built along the intermittently sandy shore—Atami, which was said to resemble Naples because of the high, steep hills above the water; Odawara, the subject of one of the best prints in Hiroshige's renowned Tokaido series; and Kamakura, the medieval capital, with its huge bronze Daibutsu, or Great Buddha, to which thousands of pilgrims still came every year to pay homage. Hidden in the wooded slopes above them were other resorts famous for their hot springs, their mountain scenery, or both—most notably Hakone, which marked the boundary of the area on the east coast known as the Kanto Plain. Towering over them all, but visible only from certain crests and beaches and at uncertain times, when capriciously unveiled by mist and cloud, stood the marvelous mountain of Fuji—to which the most apt of many million compliments was perhaps that paid by the classical poet Sokan: "a sight that should be saved for New Year's Day."

At Kamakura, the shoreline of Sagami Bay swung out to form the south side of the Miura Peninsula, dividing Sagami from Tokyo Bay. On the other side of the peninsula, perhaps ten miles as the

35

gulls fly, lay the great naval base of Yokosuka, and fifteen miles north of that was the busy port of Yokohama, which had grown up so differently from Tokyo but with even more astonishing speed. Less than seventy-five years before, when Townsend Harris, the first United States Consul to Japan, had been negotiating for a Treaty Port, Yokohama had been a village of one hundred and one houses. Now, in 1923, thanks to the commerce that had developed because of the treaty, it was a city of almost half a million, Japan's biggest port, and the heart of the silk export trade.

Unlike that of Tokyo—where foreigners outside the embassies constituted a small and essentially insignificant fraction of the population—the foreign community in Yokohama, amounting to perhaps three thousand, was not only proportionately much larger but also vastly more influential. To a considerable degree, the foreign community *was* Yokohama, or at least the city's reason for existing. Most of the more prosperous foreigners lived either in fine breezy houses on the Bluff, a long ridge running behind the city, half a mile inland, or else at the Oriental or the New Grand Hotel, on the waterfront. They had "tiffin" together at the Yokohama United Club and they attended the Union Church on Sundays unless they were away at one of the shore resorts or at Karuizawa, in the high hills north of Tokyo. On this particular Saturday, more than the usual number had stayed in town to say goodbye to friends who were leaving on the *Empress of Australia*. The *Empress* was scheduled to sail for Vancouver at midday; a few minutes before that hour, most of the seeing-off parties had left the ship and gathered on the Customs House jetty to which the big liner was moored.

One member of the foreign community who was not in the group on the jetty was a handsome young man named Antonios Pappadopoulos whose profile, with the classic straight line from nose to forehead, was as Greek as his name and who fitted particularly well into that international milieu because of his own highly cosmopolitan background. Born of Greek parents who belonged to the foreign community of Odessa, he had learned five languages and witnessed a Cossack charge in the Russian Revolution of 1906 by the time he was eleven. After college in Zurich, where he had had a trifling brush with the refugee Vladimir Ilich Lenin at a students' ball, and where he had been graduated the day Austria declared war on Serbia, Pappadopoulos had been dispatched by his father to open a branch of the family import-export firm in Vladivostok. Here he had swung a deal for a million dollars' worth of coffee for Moscow which had backfired when the 1917 Revolution had taken place, while the coffee was in transit across Siberia. That had been the end of his Vladivostok period. He had gone on to Japan, where, after a quick trip home to acquire a beautiful young wife, he had settled down to the import-export trade. In Yokohama, he devoted his ample leisure time to the sport of tennis.

Since life for Pappadopoulos, as for another noted Greek traveler before him, consisted almost exclusively of crises, it was not surprising that he had two or three of these on his hands this morning. The most perplexing one concerned a movie newsreel camera, one of three he had recently imported from Germany, which he had sold to the Imperial Court Photographer in Tokyo. The Court Photographer had brought the camera back a few days later with a pitiful tale. While he was photographing Their Imperial Majesties as they walked across the lawn of their villa at Nikko—where the Emperor was recuperating from one of his congenital nervous breakdowns—the camera had jammed. Too embarrassed to say anything about the mishap, the anguished photographer had continued to turn the crank. Now, of course, he had no film to develop; unless Pappadopoulos would take the camera back and give him an affidavit saying that it was defective, there was nothing left but to draw his *seppuku* dagger and end his life by *hara-kiri.*

37

Pappadopoulos had generously provided not only the affidavit but a brand-new camera in support of it. The first one, he found, was in fact defective: the reel fed unexposed film faster than the winder could accommodate it. The question that arose now, however—the reverse of that posed by the Cyclops—was, in effect, how to restore the camera to operational condition. Returning it to the maker was a lengthy and laborious process which might not result in any satisfactory outcome. Having it repaired in Japan was at least equally risky. Walking from his house to the tram station, where he meant to proceed to his office and pick up some money needed for settling a traffic accident case later in the day, Pappadopoulos gave serious thought to the problem. Surely something would turn up to enable him to solve it.

As THE PROJECTS of Pappadopoulos, the Prime Minister, and three million or more other people took shape on the densely populated Kanto Plain, the hands on the clock in the tower of the Meteorological Building in Tokyo, like a huge black pair of vertical shears held high above the city, closed slowly upon noon. While the hands of the clock drew together, Mayor Hidejiro Nagata of Tokyo was sitting in a soft-cushioned desk chair in his office at the City Hall. At exactly fifty-eight minutes and forty-six seconds past eleven, the electric light which hung from the ceiling of this room began to swing from side to side, and Mayor Nagata, as he later recalled, uttered an exclamation.

"Ah," he said, "earthquake!"

The Mayor could hardly have been more correct. What was causing the lamp to sway was the beginning of the Kanto *Daishinsai*, or Great Kanto Earthquake Disaster, which was not only the most destructive earthquake ever recorded but also, in all probability, the most serious natural calamity in the long and frequently calamitous history of the human race.

38

CHAPTER II

O-NAMAZU

THE ENORMOUS CATFISH

ACCORDING TO A FAMILIAR Japanese proverb, the four things which human beings should fear most are *jishin, kaminari, kaji, oyaji*—earthquake, thunderstorm, fire, and Father. While the point of this maxim is doubtless to classify paternal authority as one of the major forces of nature, the saying may, at least for foreigners, have a further significance. It shows exactly where the Japanese rate earthquakes on the scale of such forces and also serves as a reminder that, so far as nature's angrier manifestations are concerned, the Japanese are the world's ranking experts.

That the four main Japanese islands of Honshu, Kyushu, Shikoku, and Hokkaido offer mankind, at best, a somewhat precarious foothold can be readily established. To begin with, the islands comprise so many hills and mountains, most of them rocky and precipitous, that only about 15 per cent of the entire surface is arable at all, and even this meager remnant needs constant fertilization and intensive cultivation. Many of Japan's mountains—especially the famous Fuji, which serves as the geological hub of

the whole archipelago and the cynosure of most of its population—
are of volcanic origin, and some are still engaged in, or quite capable of, violent eruption. Japan has so many hot springs—well
over a thousand, and all highly esteemed for their somewhat de-
batable health-giving properties (perhaps on the principle of
contrast, since at least, unlike so many other things, they do no serious harm)—that the whole country seems to be steaming and sput-
tering like a fish-fry bar at the rush hour. As to typhoons, a dozen
or more sweep over the islands every year, usually in September
or October, causing widespread flood and havoc. Nonetheless,
despite all this, it is on the score of earthquakes that Japan most
clearly outclasses the rest of the world in what might be termed
reverse natural resources. Japan generates 15 per cent of the earthquake energy produced annually by the earth as a whole. The
runner-up, Chile, rarely does better than about twelve.

The effect of the secondary perils, among which they live, upon
the temperament and behavior of the Japanese has been exten-
sively considered elsewhere. So far as earthquakes are concerned,
however, some of the most noteworthy consequences are to be
found in the field of architecture, which, in turn, has further repercussions upon numerous Japanese mores, including the sartorial.
It can, for example, be plausibly argued that the traditional Japanese garb of kimono and *geta,* or toe-strap clogs, follows inevitably from the kind of house that Japanese people live in and, also,
that the character of the houses is largely determined by the necessity for enough earthquake resistance to accommodate the strain
of some fifteen hundred perceptible tremors every year, which is
the national average.

In constructing their houses, the Japanese long ago perceived
that there was no sense trying to make them strong enough to
withstand major shocks, such as only occur in any given spot once
in a generation or two. The idea, instead, was to make them flex-
ible enough to endure the constant minor ones and, at the same

40

time, light enough to fall down with minimum damage to themselves and their occupants in the case of the infrequent major ones. In practicing this form of residential judo, Japanese architects long ago devised a highly specialized style which is as notable for its functional practicality as for its aesthetic perfection.

The traditional Japanese house, like the houses of Southeast Asia and Malaya from which it may derive, has no subterranean foundations at all but rests instead on a few flat stones laid carefully on the surface of the ground. The framework and walls are made of light strips of resinous wood, with or without a thin plaster covering. The partitions are sliding wood-and-paper panels. The floors are mats made out of woven rice-straw. That these apparently perishable ingredients are in fact astonishingly durable is due to several other circumstances, of which at least two are especially relevant. One is the skill of Japanese carpenters who, instead of using nails, since these would presently be shaken loose, join their timbers by means of intricate and ingenious mortise. The other is the custom of making the soft, smooth *tatami* floors serve all the purposes for which most other nations require much massive furniture. This is a custom for which the kimono, being adapted to floor-sitting, and geta, which can be readily slipped off at the front door, are far more appropriate than European clothes or shoes. That, in the hundred years since Japan became accessible to foreign influences, the latter have gained considerable acceptance may prove less that they are suitable than that the Japanese —in their eagerness to overlook no possible advantage from foreign influences—are prepared to go to unwise extremes.

Foreign visitors to Japan who have never felt really severe quakes and are thus not much in awe of them often find the minor ones diverting experiences. The Japanese, in whom the dread of such events has been conveyed from one generation to another, take them much more seriously. In a severe earthquake, they believe that the best thing to do is to get outdoors as fast as possible—

taking care to avoid the falling tiles which, on such occasions, rain down from the roofs of their dwellings. If there isn't time to get outdoors—and preferably to a bamboo grove—the safest place is under a doorway or, failing that, at the side of a room, preferably an upstairs one. Since in a severe quake the flimsy framework supporting the upper story is likely to break, causing the floor to crash down on the rooms below, the second story is considered the safer in houses which have two.

While it is true that Japanese architecture represents an ingenious defense against earthquakes, it would be wrong to suggest that it is by any means a completely successful one. Fireplaces and furnaces are omitted from Japanese houses since both would involve the hazard of chimneys. Instead, the Japanese use charcoal braziers of various types—most commonly *shichirin* for cooking and *hibachi* for heating, both of which also have serious drawbacks. One is that they are not especially efficient. The other is that in earthquakes they are likely to tip over and spill live coals on the tatami mats. Since Japanese houses are, in effect, tinderboxes which could not be made more inflammable if they were expressly designed for burning, and since in severe quakes householders make a point of running outdoors immediately, the very measures employed to avert inconvenience during minor earthquakes invite destruction by fire in a major one. The danger is, moreover, vastly enhanced by the traditional plan of Japanese towns and cities, whereby the tinderbox houses are crowded close together over wide areas in which the only thoroughfares are alleys just wide enough to provide the drafts required for a major conflagration.

Assembling practical hints about what to do when an earthquake hits and how to build houses that will, so to speak, roll with the punch is by no means Japan's only important contribution to the general field of earthquake lore. On the contrary, since the dawn of their history, the Japanese have been making diligent efforts to find out more about earthquakes in general and more about what causes them in particular in the hope of being able eventually to predict them. The Japanese government began to keep complete records of important earthquakes in A.D. 481 and has maintained them diligently ever since.

In the old days—unlike the Indians, who thought earthquakes were caused by an underground cow, or the Chinese, who credited a subterranean turtle—the Japanese believed that quakes were caused by an enormous catfish, lying curled up under the sea, upon whose back all four of the islands rather precariously reposed. When the catfish wiggled, the earth shook. Some etymologists, upon rather sketchy grounds, have argued that the archaic Japanese word for earthquake, which was *nai*, had some common root with the word for catfish, which, with its appropriate prefix, is *o-namazu*. The catfish was supposed to lie in such a tight curl that his head and tail were contiguous under a place called Kashima. A large rock there marks the spot.

While the world's best seismologists no longer think it probable that earthquakes are caused by catfish, cows, or turtles, and while, since 1923, they have been studying the matter much harder than ever before, it cannot be said that they are yet entirely clear about what *does* cause them. The most seismologists will say is that earthquakes represent the release of potential energy, or stress, originally accumulated in the earth's crust as the result of the differential between the earth's hot interior and its relatively cool exterior. Such stress seems most likely to develop in regions where mountainous land areas are reasonably close to fairly deep parts of the sea. Several such regions exist on the perimeter of the Pacific, and Japan conforms especially well to the specifications. Mount Fuji, over 12,000 feet high, is only about a hundred miles away from an underwater trench off Japan's east coast—called the Tuscarora Deep after the United States warship that first sounded it in 1874—which is over 30,000 feet deep.

As to the widely entertained theory that all earthquakes are

43

caused by shifts or slides along well-defined splits or "faults" on the earth's surface, this is, at best, a plausible half-truth. It owes its prevalence, in the United States especially, to the fact that the great San Francisco quake of 1906 did indeed occur along the renowned San Andreas fault and that a good many other quakes have occurred along fault lines also. In fact, earthquakes are of two kinds: those that occur along fault lines and those that don't. Both kinds are numerous; and even in the case of the ones that do occur on faults, no one can be sure whether it was the fault that caused the commotion or the other way around. In Japan, both sorts of earthquake abound.

ONE THING that has speeded up the gathering of earthquake lore since 1923 is that the subject has lately been studied more as a geophysical than a geological discipline; and much of the new knowledge relates to the motion caused by earthquakes and how best to measure it. Earthquakes, nowadays, are graded on the Richter scale, which was devised in 1935 by Professor Charles F. Richter of the California Institute of Technology at Pasadena, who is probably the top United States authority on such matters. This scale represents the maximum displacement which would have been recorded on a standard Wood-Anderson seismograph placed one hundred kilometers from the epicenter—which is a point on the earth's surface directly above the center of the disturbance. The scale ascends from −1, with each digit signifying ten times as much magnitude as the one below it. On the Richter scale, the Great Kanto Earthquake, like the San Francisco quake of 1906, rated 8.3, or a bit less than the Chilean quake of 1960. From the practical and humanistic—as distinguished from the seismological—approach, however, the main thing about an earthquake is not its magnitude so much as the proximity of its point of origin to a major population center—since intensity, as distinct from original magnitude, drops rapidly in ratio to distance from this point.

One mildly reassuring characteristic of earthquakes is that the similarity to each other in magnitude of the three just mentioned, is by no means a coincidence but, on the contrary, seems to betoken a sort of ceiling on the size of such disturbances. Why such a ceiling should exist is hard to say, except that the amount of stress the earth can accumulate apparently has certain limits like the amount of moisture or electrical charge that can be stored in a cloud before it produces lightning or rain. In any event, while there have been nearly two hundred quakes of 7.9 or more on the Richter scale since 1900, there have been none greater than 8.9; and judging from all the numerous available signs, none of the earthquakes that occurred before 1900 were any bigger either.

Since the magnitude of the shock is limited, the area which can be devastated by it is also sharply circumscribed. According to Professor Chuji Tsuboi of Tokyo University, who is currently Japan's leading authority on such matters, the principle here can be demonstrated by taking a good-sized box full of sand and giving it a sharp rap on one side. Sand in the vicinity of the point rapped will be disturbed but not all the sand in the box; and the earth's crust, composed of materials which are analogous to the sand grains, reacts more or less the same way. Thus, even quakes which rate 8 or more on the Richter scale will rarely be very destructive beyond a distance of some two hundred kilometers from their epicenters. As a matter of fact, truly sophisticated experts like Professor Tsuboi are much less interested in how big earthquakes can get, since this is already fairly well established, than in how small, since really tiny earthquakes are handier to study and reveal a lot about the big ones. The smallest that he has been able to record so far was a little minnow detected a few years ago on the side of Mt. Tsukuba, whose magnitude on the Richter scale was −1. This dwarf disturbance took place within one cubic yard—about the measure of a good-sized Japanese bonsai, or table-landscape.

The main reason so little is known about earthquakes is, of course, that seismology is still a relatively new branch of science, dating back only to the development of the seismograph, or—as some experts prefer to call it—seismometer. To be sure, the Chinese had developed the first seismo*scope* by A.D. 132, in the ingenious form of eight dragons in a ring, each holding a copper ball which, when dislodged by a quake, would drop into the mouth of a waiting toad. However, while this was doubtless the most decorative and amusing device ever developed for the purpose, and while it did indicate very roughly the magnitude of minor quakes, it was not wholly satisfactory as a means of record or comparison. For this, the world had to wait until late in the nineteenth century, when an Englishman named Robert Mallet wrote a two-volume study of the Neapolitan earthquake of 1857, which got the science off to a good start.

Really effective seismographs, which operate on the pendulum principle to determine the extent and direction of the earth's motion at a given point, and which consist of three needles to register east-west, north-south and up-down motion on revolving drums, were not developed until about 1880, first in japan and later in Europe. Seismographs record what are essentially three different types of earthquake wave: two of these are vibrations spreading through the earth from the actual center; the third type is an undulation spreading along the top of the earth from the epicenter. The interval between the arrival times of the two first types establishes the earthquake's distance from the recorder, just as the interval between the lightning flash and the thunderclap establishes the thunderstorm's distance from the hearer. Records from three or more well-separated seismographs thus serve to locate the origin of any earthquake with reasonable accuracy.

When an earthquake starts, the subterranean vibrations, both varieties of which are usually called "preliminary tremors," always arrive first since they take a more expeditious route, but they are not usually the ones that do the damage. This is caused by the surface waves of which the violence is naturally more or less proportionate to their distance from the epicenter. As a convenient rule of thumb, such waves, popularly known as the "main shock," are normally something like ten times as strong as the preliminary tremors.

As to the accompanying effects of earthquakes—about which more mythology has developed than about any other phase of the subject—these are likely to include not only routine matters like landslides, upheavals and breakage, but also earthquake or tidal waves, more correctly called *tsunami*, weird lights flickering around in the sky, loud roaring noises, and fissures that open up and may or may not close again. Contrary to popular belief, these fissures almost never "swallow up" anybody or anything. A cow supposedly swallowed up in the San Francisco quake was found later to have been merely a foolish creature who hurt herself by stumbling into a fissure and was later, for the sake of convenience, buried there, with the tip of her tail sticking out. In the severe Fukui quake of 1948, a Mrs. Sadako Nankyo, while working in a rice paddy, fell into a fissure which did, in fact, close before she could scramble out again. This made her the only victim of such a mishap in authenticated earthquake history. While it is true that being buried in landslides or sealed up inside of caves are more or less ordinary earthquake hazards, few seismologists believe legends like the one about the ten thousand members of a North African tribe called "Sons of Busienba," who were supposed to have been enclosed by a fissure after the Lisbon earthquake of 1775.

The noise made by an earthquake in a big city is, of course, mainly the noise of many houses and the things in them rattling or falling down. In rural areas, the earthquake itself may cause audible sound waves of a lower level, though these are usually hard to distinguish from the sounds made by secondary moving objects, such as stones or trees. As to the lights that are supposed to flicker in the sky during a major quake, few people have ever seen these and no one has the slightest notion what might cause them. Indeed, they belong rather in the flying-saucer area of scientific research and might be regarded as altogether mythical except for the fact that they were actually sketched by a witness during the Izu Peninsula earthquake of 1930. Even this sketch might be dismissed as a surrealist abstraction were it not for the fact that such lights have been frequently reported elsewhere; and that an old Japanese wood-block print dating back to the Tokugawa period, with which the Izu artist could hardly have been acquainted, is an almost exact replica or prototype.

As to tsunami—which British seismologists for some odd reason of their own prefer to spell "tsunamis," even in the singular, although no Japanese word ends with "s" even in the plural—these are sometimes just as dangerous as the quake itself, or even more so. Californians, who from time to time may have seen the water sloshed out of their swimming pools by major or even minor earthquakes, may suppose that tidal waves represent more or less the same kind of activity on a larger scale, but nothing could be further from the truth. Such sloshing around by the contents of pools or, for that matter, cocktail glasses, is what scientists call a seiche; and while seiches can be and, indeed, are caused by all earthquakes, in everything from medicine bottles to small bays, they have nothing to do with tsunami, which result from sudden upheavals, depressions, or landslides on the ocean floor.

One comforting thing about tsunami is that they do not, as is often supposed, travel across the ocean in the form of cliffs of water. While they travel for long distances and extremely fast—up to about 500 miles an hour—they normally do so in the form of long, gradual swells, sometimes measuring hundreds of miles from trough to crest, which ocean liners and even fishing boats may ride easily, frequently without even being aware of them. It is only as they approach shore—especially a gradual beach in a V-shaped bay, like many in the Hawaiian Islands, which suffer severely from such waves—that they become more vertical as they race toward land like sudden tides that may rise many feet above the normal high-water mark. Whether or not an earthquake will be followed by tsunami depends entirely on what the quake does to the sea bottom. The worst ever experienced in Japan was one caused by the century's most severe shock to date, an 8.5 one off the Sanriku coast in 1933. The shock proved relatively harmless, but the tsunami reached a maximum height of seventy-five feet and wiped out numerous small towns and villages, along with some 27,000 of their inhabitants.

Like that of tsunami, the predictability of earthquakes is on an exceedingly inexact basis. Anyone can predict, with some assurance, that there will be another major earthquake in or near Tokyo within a century; that there will be a major earthquake in Japan within the next five years; and that there will be a noticeable earthquake somewhere within the next minute. Such forecasts, however, are merely applications of the law of averages; and more precise clues as to the exact time and place of major disturbances in the future are still sadly lacking. One of the few relatively successful efforts in this field was that made about the Great Kanto Earthquake a year or so before it happened by Japan's then leading seismologist, the late Professor Fusakichi Omori. Himself a student of the renowned Professor John Milne, who had come to Japan in the eighties after working with Mallet in London, Omori had devoted a lifetime of worldwide research to his subject and based his forecasts upon two major lines of investigation. One was a convenient cliff on the Japanese coast, which over the centuries had apparently been raised out of the sea in four successive stages, at each of which a certain species of small shellfish began nibbling holes in it above the waterline. Assuming that each elevation was caused by a sizable earthquake and that the shellfish nibbled at a constant rate, it had been possible to deduce precisely when the major quakes in the Tokyo area had occurred ever since A.D. 33. By combining this knowledge with his own study of smaller quakes in the vicinity over the previous decades, Omori had been saying for several years, and said again in an article in 1921, that something might be doing presently in the area of Tokyo Bay.

The only trouble with Omori's prediction was that almost nobody paid enough attention to it, including the learned professor himself. Deceived by a reasonably severe shock in 1922, which he mistook for the major disturbance that he had been anticipating for so many years, Omori announced, somewhat prematurely, that Tokyo would probably not experience another bad quake in the foreseeable future. This optimistic prognosis was preserved for posterity in the *Japanese Yearbook* for 1924, which also described the earthquake that had actually occurred in a special supplement of more than two hundred pages, added later. Meanwhile, just when it would have been most appropriate for him to be in Tokyo, Professor Omori sailed off to attend a conference about earthquakes in Australia, thus missing the chance of a long lifetime that ended only two months later. About the only person in Japan or anywhere else who gave his original prediction the credence which it most assuredly deserved was a United States engineer named Paul Van Zandt, who, as technical representative of a Japanese-owned cement company, lived in a commodious house on the Yokohama Bluff. Alarmed not only by the Omori prediction but also by the same 1922 quake which had misled the professor, Van Zandt moved his family back to Chicago and had been comfortably settled there for just two weeks when the 1923 quake completely demolished his former house and killed all its new tenants.

THAT THE GREAT KANTO EARTHQUAKE of 1923 was not only the worst earthquake but the worst natural calamity of any sort ever experienced by the human race is a statement that may require justification. To begin with, of course, it is not true at all, unless one includes the consequences together with the quake; however, to do so seems logical since a mere shaking-up hurts nobody and it is only the consequences of the shaking upon other objects that does any damage anyway. On this basis, few other earthquakes have been even remotely comparable. The maximum estimate of the death toll in the San Francisco quake and fire, for example, was about 1,400, or 1 per cent of the number who died in, or just after, the Great Kanto Earthquake; and the destruction of property was roughly proportionate.

While the Kanto earthquake completely outclasses San Francisco's in its destructive effects, history does include a few others which may rival it. One of these was the great Lisbon earthquake, which occurred at 9:30 in the morning of November 1, 1755, when almost everyone was attending All Saints' Day Mass. The churches collapsed on them and the earthquake was followed by prodigious tsunami, which helped produce a death toll of some 60,000. Others were the Edo earthquake of 1703, for which the figure usually given is 200,000, the Indian earthquake of 1737, supposed to have killed 300,000 in and around Calcutta, and the Shansi, China, earthquake of 1556, of which the legendary total of 800,000 is the largest of all.

In fact, while the 1556 quake must have been highly lethal since it occurred in country where most of the inhabitants lived in caves, it also occurred in China, where most of the inhabitants also like to exaggerate. Really vast earthquake destruction requires a major fire, and this requires a major metropolis. The chances are that the 1556 quake, while plenty big enough to provide all the seismoscopic toads with a mouthful, was less destructive than the Kanto one in terms of human life. Both the Indian earthquake of 1737, and the 1703 one of Edo, when Edo was considerably smaller, must be ruled out on the same grounds. In modern times, the closest rival was perhaps the Chinese quake of December 16, 1920, which was said to have killed 180,000 cave-dwelling residents of Kansu and Shansi. Here again, however, the statistics are unreliable; and certainly the Kanto earthquake seems unlikely to have been rivaled in prehistoric times when there were comparatively few people on the earth and their settlements consequently smaller. Since an earthquake is the most destructive kind of accident that can happen, it seems logical to suppose that the Kanto quake was the most calamitous accident on record.

According to the numerous seismographs in the Tokyo area, the point of origin of the Great Kanto Earthquake was some ten miles north of the island of Oshima and also some ten miles beneath the surface. However, beyond this meager data, the local seismographs, seismoscopes or seismometers have little to contribute. The reason for this is that, even if by no means the most severe ever recorded, the quake was plenty severe enough to exceed the capacity of all the instruments in the area—since these were naturally adjusted to make precise recordings of the frequent minor earthquakes, rather than to attempt to execute a rough sketch of a mammoth one. Needles registered the preliminary tremors accurately, but the surface waves knocked them all off their drums immediately. The only source of information about what happened afterward was eyewitnesses' accounts. As might be expected, these vary considerably—partly because the quake differed from place to place and partly because no two observers reacted to it in the same way.

One point on which observers are fairly unanimous is that, after the first few seconds, even the preliminary tremors were as violent as the main shock of an ordinary quake. From this circumstance alone the more knowledgeable sensed that the great Kanto one was going to be something quite as special as, in fact, it proved to be. The main shock taxed descriptive powers. One witness said it felt as though the earth had been pulled out from under him like a rug. Another compared it to riding on a train that had gone off the tracks and was bouncing along on the ties. Probably the most accurate report was that provided by Professor Akitsune Imamura, who inherited Omori's mantle as Japan's senior seismologist a short time later, and who had the advantage over his predecessor of being seated in the Seismological Institute at Tokyo when the quake began:

At first, the movement was rather slow and feeble, so that I did not take it to be the forerunner of so big a shock. As usual, I began to esti-mate the duration of the preliminary tremors. . . . Soon, the vibration became large and after three or four seconds from the commencement I felt the shock very strong indeed. Seven or eight seconds passed, and the building was shaking to an extraordinary extent, but I considered these movements not yet to be the principal portion. When I calculated these movements the twelfth second from the start, there arrived a very big vibration which I took at once as the beginning of the principal portion. Now the motion, instead of becoming less and less as usual, went on to increase its intensity very quickly, and after four or five seconds I felt it to have reached its strongest. During this epoch, the tiles were showering down from the roof, making a loud noise, and I wondered whether the building could stand or not. I realized the direc-tion of the principal movements distinctly and found them to have been about northwest or southeast. During the following ten seconds the motion, though still violent, became somewhat less severe and its char-acter was gradually changing into slower but bigger vibrations. For the next few minutes we felt the undulations like those which we experi-ence on a boat in windy weather, having now and then been threatened by severe aftershocks. After five minutes from the beginning, I stood up and went over to see the instruments.

As in the case of most major earthquakes, the Kanto one was followed by numerous aftershocks of gradually diminishing violence and frequency. Some of these aftershocks appeared to come from the same source and some from other sources. In all, 237 were felt on the afternoon and evening of September 1, 92 on September 2, and a total of over 1,200 during the rest of the month. One violent aftershock occurred about fifteen minutes after the main one. The next day, at 11:46, or almost exactly 24 hours later, there occurred an even stronger one that almost equaled the original on the Richter scale. Tokyo residents began to wonder if a major earthquake at noon was to be a regular event on the diurnal schedule, like sunrise and sunset.

Within seconds of the first shock, the consequences of the disaster began to be apparent. These included landslides, tsunami, flashes of light, roaring noises, fires, explosions, the collapse of hundreds of thousands of houses and, later on, death on a scale never equaled before and never likely to be equaled again, unless, of course, the world goes in for nuclear warfare, in which case it will doubtless be vastly exceeded. Nonetheless, even when compared with a nuclear war, the Great Kanto Earthquake may have had a special horror of its own. In war, death and destruction are to be expected. People are somewhat prepared to be brave and, perhaps even more important, thoroughly prepared to be angry. Earthquakes occur, on the contrary, when people are not prepared for anything much, except, for example, as in the case of the Kanto one, to sit down to lunch.

Wars arouse patriotic fervor and a sense of purpose, but earthquakes are more likely to produce gloom, despair and inertia. They generate resentment, but this is not directed toward anyone in particular; it is a rage completely at loose ends and one which seeks a target. What the subconscious is to the mind of an individual, the earth itself may be to mankind. Earthquakes thus seem not to be part of the world of intentional cause and effect, the world of conscious history—in which, as a rule, they get scant attention.

They seem rather to belong to the world of nightmare, which we can forget upon awakening. In fact, however, earthquakes are not nightmares, nor are they composed of mere statistics. They are entirely real and they may involve large numbers of living beings.

CHAPTER III

KANTO DAI-SHINSAI

GREAT EARTHQUAKE DISASTER ON THE KANTO PLAIN

According to reasonably well-founded but necessarily imprecise estimates made after both events, the shock of the Great Kanto Earthquake—as distinct from the immense conflagrations that followed it—destroyed only about 1 per cent of the 500,000 or so buildings in Tokyo. Tokyo, however, was 57 miles from the epicenter; in Yokohama, 17 miles to the south and therefore that much closer, there was a proportionate difference. There, more than 12 per cent of the 100,000 or so buildings crashed with the main shock—causing that much greater immediate loss of life and accelerating the start of the numerous fires that broke out in both cities within the next few minutes.

Even Yokohama was by no means the place hardest hit. This distinction was reserved for some of the smaller towns on the shore of Sagami Bay which were not only much closer to the epicenter but also—as the cities on the shore of Tokyo Bay were not—exposed to tsunami of varying size. Among these towns, the effects of the shock were perhaps most noteworthy at Kamakura, which experienced both a fire and a tsunami as well as a shock of top intensity. There the shock alone destroyed some 85 per cent of the houses or a total of around 2,500; fires consumed half of the remainder. Deaths averaged about one person to ten houses demolished by the quake. One of the more noteworthy was that of the nineteen-year-old Princess Sakiko Yamashina who was in a condition of advanced pregnancy. She was being visited by her doctor when the roof of the house crashed down, killing both herself and the physician.

Among the many other eminent residents of Kamakura was the widely revered Prince Masayoshi Matsukata who, in failing health at the advanced age of eighty-eight, spent most of his time resting in his villa, where he was attended by one or more nurses. Prince Matsukata was one of the most significant links between the two dramatically different eras in Japan's recent history. At the time of the Meiji Restoration in 1868, he had been one of the group of young and rebellious samurai who had helped to overthrow the Tokugawa shoguns, thus bringing Japan overnight into the modern world. Awarded the highest title in his new realm by the Emperor, the Prince had had a rapid rise in the government and for the next four decades exerted major power on the political scene, holding office frequently as Finance Minister and five times as Prime Minister. An amazing streak of personal good luck had on several occasions saved him from assassinations such as those that ended the careers of several of his less fortunate contemporaries.

On the morning of September 1, the old Prince was reclining on the tatami in a room on the ground floor; in a room directly above him, his twenty-three-year-old son, Saburo, just out of Kyoto University, was seated by the window, reading Victor Hugo's *Les Misérables*. When the quake struck—owing to the proximity of the epicenter, there was practically no period of preliminary tremor—the shock was so violent that Saburo had the impression that a stray shell fired by the Japanese fleet, which often held maneuvers in Sagami Bay, must have struck the house. The next thing that he was aware of was the sensation of recovering consciousness and finding himself on the roof of the house, which appeared to be resting directly on the ground. How he had achieved this position, Saburo never learned for sure; his deduction was that in the collapse of the house, he had been simultaneously knocked unconscious and pushed through a gap in the roof, which had closed again when it hit the ground. Despite a deep gash in the side of his right leg, he hobbled down the slope of the roof and stepped off onto the ground.

With three of the house servants who had emerged unhurt from the crash, Saburo managed to raise one corner of the roof and prop it up sufficiently to enable them to start groping about underneath for the remains of his father. To their amazement, they found that the old Prince's traditional good luck had held. Instead of being crushed in the wreckage, he was totally uninjured, as was his nurse. Both had been situated on a rectangle of floor space which happened to coincide exactly with a square frame of heavy ceiling beams. These had impeded the fall of the upper story and sustained its weight about a foot above them. The Prince crawled calmly out and soon felt well enough to have his lunch in the unquiet garden, which—like all the rest of the Kanto area—was quivering with the first of the protracted aftershocks. Saburo fared less well; by the time one of Kamakura's overworked doctors could attend to his leg wound, he had suffered serious loss of blood and a lingering infection followed. He was barely able to walk to the funeral when his father died peacefully of old age a full year later.

The Matsukata villa was on high ground above Kamakura Bay, an indentation of Sagami Bay. A few hundred yards to the west, in a house much closer to the beach, lived another notable, the retired diplomat Count Hirokichi Mutsu, whose English wife was a writer well known for her book of essays about Kamakura and its history. The Mutsus' only son, Ian, was in his room on the second floor of this house, getting ready to spend the afternoon fishing for sea bass. High tide, when they were supposed to bite best, was at one o'clock; he meant to start out at a few minutes after twelve. The shock of the quake caused the Mutsu house to collapse but not so completely as to prevent Mutsu from crawling out of a window into a tree. When he slid down to the ground, he found his father also unhurt but concerned that one or more of the servants might still be trapped inside. The Count dispatched Ian to look for his mother, who had gone swimming, while he himself stayed to investigate the wreckage.

Ian started out along the beach, but before he had gone many steps he noticed something strange that was happening to the water in the bay. The tide should have been coming in, but instead it was retreating from the beach at an unprecedented speed. Within a few minutes, while he watched, it receded farther than he had ever seen it go before, even at dead-low tide. Rocks normally almost submerged were now altogether above water; others that he had never seen before were sticking out above the surface. Suddenly Ian remembered everything he had heard about the tsunami that often follow earthquakes. At that same moment, he saw, stretched across the narrow entrance of the little bay, what looked like a long level wall of water rushing in toward him at a menacing speed.

Ian began to run—first up the slope of the beach away from the water and then up the steeper hillside above the beach. He crossed the highway, on which there was a car parked at an intersection, and called to the driver, who started his motor and began backing the car, apparently in order to turn into an uphill side road. Ian continued to run, up this side road and away from the shoreline. When he was perhaps fifty yards up the road and thirty feet higher than the beach, he paused and looked back.

The tsunami was now almost at the beach—about fifty feet offshore—and it appeared considerably bigger than when he had first seen it. At shorter range, he could see that it was about fifteen feet high and shaped less like a wall than like a steep ridge running straight across the bay. The wave never formed a crest and broke; instead it gushed up onto the beach in the form of a great swell. Ian heard the water hissing and gurgling into the streets of the lower part of the town and funneling into the mouth of the Nameri River, along the bank of which ran the road he was on. He waited where he was for perhaps a quarter of an hour, to see whether the wave would be repeated. When it was not, he started back to the house. On the way he passed the parked car; the wave had tipped it over on its side and the chauffeur was standing helplessly beside it. At the house, he found that his mother—who had also seen the tsunami in time to escape to high ground—had returned safely. The wave had not reached the house, and no one in it—unlike some two hundred other inhabitants of the town—had been mortally injured.

The tsunami which Ian Mutsu saw at Kamakura represented a fairly classic example of this phenomenon. The little bay at Kamakura has the horseshoe shape and the sloping floor required to give such a wave increasing height and profile as it rushes toward the land. Kamakura, however, was still some thirty miles north of the epicenter of the quake; and while this distance is not so determining a factor in the behavior of tsunami as it is in the behavior of the ground, it is one of the many elements that may influence them. As estimated later from measurement of its high-water mark, the wave at Kamakura reached a maximum height of about sixteen feet. Farther down the coast of Sagami Bay, it reached considerably greater heights; and at several places there were two waves in close succession. One of these places was the resort of Ito, where the waves carried 100-ton fishing boats a quarter of a mile inland. More dangerous than the waves themselves was their undertow, which dragged some three hundred houses out into the sea. At Ito, however—which had experienced a much bigger wave in 1703—the townsfolk escaped without a fatality. At Atami, ten miles farther north, the tsunami reached its maximum height of thirty-six feet and there one hundred and sixty people drowned.

In Atami, Ito, and some other coastal towns, the damage done by the tsunami rivaled or exceeded that which had been done a few minutes before by the quake and that which was to be done in the ensuing hours by the fire. In Atami, for example, the number of houses that collapsed during the shock happened to coincide exactly with the number of dwellings that were smashed or carried away by the tsunami—155 for each, amounting to about a quarter of the town's total. In Ito, the quake had demolished only about 200 houses, or a tenth of the town. However, in both of these and in some smaller communities, the tsunami may have saved as many houses as it destroyed, by extinguishing fires. It was not in these towns but a little farther west, near the center of the crescent of Sagami Bay, that the quake itself reached maximum intensity and accomplished results that were most impressive compared with its after-effects.

In the town of Odawara, where there had been about 5,000 buildings before the quake, only about 250 remained standing the next day; half of the destruction had been done by the quake. In the two nearby villages of Soga and Shimosoga, the quake destroyed 90 and 97 per cent, respectively, of all the dwellings; the hamlets were wrecked so completely that neither had enough left in it to provide fuel for a destructive fire. The most completely wrecked village of all was Nebukawa, at the mouth of the Nebukawa River, near Atami. Into the narrow, precipitous gorge formed by this little river, the quake poured landslides from the hills on each side, thus forming a sort of glacier of mud some 200 yards wide and 50 feet deep at the mouth of the river. The landslides killed some 300 of the inhabitants and the mud glacier pushed most of the village into the bay, burying the site of the remnants beyond hope of excavation.

The railroad station at Nebukawa, notched precariously into the side of the steep slope rising from the water, had the distinction of being the scene of the most calamitous single consequence of the earthquake itself, as distinct from its after-effects. Just coming to a standstill at the Nebukawa platform—where it was to await the up-train from Atami and points south—was the train from Tokyo on which Tatsuo Shiraishi and his eight fellow drivers were riding to their happy weekend at Ito. At the first shock, the hillside above the station gave way with a deafening roar in a landslide which brushed the train, the station and everyone in them down a hundred-and-fifty-foot precipice into the sea.

Tatsuo was one of the very few passengers on the train who survived its crash into the water. In some way which he was later unable to recall, he managed to emerge and to reach the surface. Of those few who did, he was, so far as the records show, the only one who reached the shore alive. On struggling to the beach—he barely knew how to swim and nearly drowned on the way—he took stock of his condition. Except for a few severe bruises and a head cut, he was as well as he had been before starting his nap a few minutes before. Tatsuo rested a bit, chatting with a few dazed survivors of the village of Nebukawa who had run to the beach to escape the landslide. Then since there seemed to be nothing else to do, he clambered up the steep bank to the tracks and started walking back in the direction of Tokyo. The Tokyo train that was to have met his train at Nebukawa never caught up with him. This, by good fortune, had been in a tunnel during the landslide—which, however, blocked the tunnel ahead of the train. Some of the passengers were injured when the engine plowed into the obstruction, but the rest were able to get out of their cars, walk back, and emerge from the tunnel at the other end.

An odd thing that Tatsuo Shiraishi noticed as he began a homeward hike that took him three days was that the sparrows in the
orange groves along the way seemed for some reason to be
grounded. They kept hopping about, but each time one attempted
to take off, it could barely manage to flutter as far as the lower
limbs of the nearest tree. A few seconds later, there would be
another tremor and the birds who had flapped their way into the
trees would fall off and flutter helplessly back to the ground.

Various other observers noted strange behavior on the part of
other birds, beasts and even fish. According to the crews of Sagami
Bay trawlers, hundreds of *shige*—a species of large bottom-feeding
fish—floated up to the surface the day after the quake. They had
been killed, apparently, in the same way that trout may be killed by
throwing a stick of dynamite in a stream, by a sudden and extreme
change in the water pressure. Just before the quake, pheasants
were heard crowing wildly in various sections of the countryside;
and an observer in Yokohama said that he had been able to
gauge the severity of the aftershocks by the whinnying of a certain
horse tethered in a field. Apparently better constructed for seismological purposes than bipeds, this frightened animal would signal
each shock just before it became perceptible to human sensibilities.
The louder the whinny, the more severe would be the ensuing
tremor.

AMONG THE SHIPS moored inside the breakwater in the harbor
of Yokohama on September 1 was the Blue Funnel liner *Philoctetes*,
one of whose passengers had a first-rate panorama view of the
proceedings. These he later recorded in admirably vivid fashion for
anonymous publication in the Kobe *Chronicle*:

Precisely at noon, the writer was seated in his cabin reading when he
was startled by the violent shaking of the entire ship. The motion was
similar to that experienced when one rides on an "electric horse" gen-

erally found in the gymnasium of large liners. This peculiar sensation
was so insistent and so violent that he thought the boilers of the vessel
were on the point of exploding. Everyone on board was alarmed. Someone—perhaps it was one of the Japanese winchmen, more experienced
in these things—suggested it was an earthquake. There was no possibility of an error. The first shock lasted possibly a full minute but it
seemed like five. The decks of the vessel were vibrating in a most alarming manner and it was feared the shock might break her back. This was
on a 14,000 ton liner, on the water, which is supposed to be the safest
place to be during an earthquake—what it must have been ashore, must
be left to another, with the experience, to describe.

About a minute following this lengthy shock, a yellow cloud—very
thin at first but growing in size every second—rose from the land; from
behind the houses, the docks, the hills beyond. This cloud formed a
continuous strip all around the bay, growing in size and deepening in
color, travelling at great speed toward the north. This cloud was doubtless caused by the dust from collapsing buildings etc., and soon filled
the atmosphere.

People on the ships stood by and waited. The plight of the people
ashore can only be imagined.

From where the writer was, great damage was evident immediately
after the first shock. The buildings ashore could be seen, from the distance, to have materially altered due to collapse. The two lengths of the
breakwater forming the Eastern boundary of Yokohama harbour had
somewhat changed. A portion of each length, forming the gateway
through which ships come and go, had entirely disappeared. A house on
the North section of the breakwater which was used as a quarantine
station, had crumbled into a shapeless mass. . . .

Contrary to the supposition of the alert observer on the *Philoctetes,* the extent of the catastrophe, as distinct from its intensity, was not quite as readily discernible in the city as it was
from a vantage point offshore. Passengers on the *Empress of
Australia,* looking down from the rail to watch the gangplank go
up, saw the Customs House jetty begin to rock in what some of
them may have momentarily mistaken for an illusion caused by

the motion of the ship. In this case, the pier's motion was not an illusion; as the piles that supported it gave way, both ends crumpled and slid into the water, leaving the crowd of visitors marooned on an island in the middle.

In the crowd on the pier was an eleven-year-old American boy named Robert Blum who, with his brother, had been on hand to say goodbye to one of their schoolmates at St. Joseph's on the Bluff who was returning to the United States. The violent shaking of the pier caused Blum first to lose his footing and then, in regaining it, to lose his straw hat. Being of the stiff-brimmed boater type then fashionable, this rolled across the now steeply slanting surface of the pier toward the water. In the confusion of the moment—full of dust and the enormous noise of the city crashing into ruins—it somehow seemed important to Blum that he at least regain his hat. As he scrambled and stooped to get it, he heard a man near him say in an excited tone, "Another quake like that and there won't be a Yokohama!"

Another quake would have been superfluous, but the crowd on the pier was not yet fully aware of that. Blum retrieved his hat. The brim was slightly twisted but he put it on. A few minutes later, with the rest of the crowd, he was herded across the pier onto a barge. There someone mentioned the possibility of a tidal wave and the word passed around quickly, making the barge seem suddenly precarious. The crowd left it and boarded another ship, the French Messageries Maritimes liner *André LeBon* which was moored to the same pier but on the side opposite the *Empress*. It was the custom for French mail ships to have their engines overhauled at Yokohama, between the outbound and the homeward passage, and the *André LeBon*'s were, for that reason, inoperable. Later that afternoon, to avoid the menace of the fires on shore, she got a small boat to carry a line to a harbor buoy and winched herself away from the pier. Blum passed that night on board. The

next day, he and his brother were transferred to another ship, the
P. & O. liner *Dongola*, which took them to Kobe, along with many
other refugees.

One of the Blums' schoolmates at St. Joseph's was a boy by the
euphonious name of Dante Dentici. Instead of seeing the *Empress*
off, his plan for the afternoon was to go to the movies. He was at
home, in the process of persuading his father to give him a one-
yen note for this purpose, when the earthquake struck. The senior
Dentici, an enterprising Italian who had come to Yokohama some
forty years before to open the town's first European bakery, was
thrown to the floor; the ceiling crashed down; Dante Dentici was
pinned in the wreckage with a broken jaw. His father pulled him
out but it took an hour or so to do it. By that time, Yokohama
was burning in a hundred places, and, like thousands of others,
the Denticis headed for the waterfront.

Among the important buildings that collapsed in the first shock
was the Yokohama United Club. Usually crowded by noon every
day, it was on this occasion practically deserted because of the sailing of the *Empress*, but the half-dozen members who were in
the building were all killed when it fell. Among them was the
club's distinguished librarian, W. B. Mason, a close friend of Laf-
cadio Hearn and himself the co-author of *A Japanese Handbook,*
who had stepped into the library from the veranda a moment before. The two men with whom he had been chatting there both
survived—one by jumping into the street, the other by stepping
into the club's doorway, which protected him from the falling rubble that piled up around him.

With the exception of the Yokohama Specie Bank and a very
few others, all the major buildings of Yokohama crashed into
ruins the same instant. One of the few exceptions was the Grand
Hotel, Yokohama's best, which, being a wooden structure, collapsed in a more leisurely fashion than its brick or stone equivalents including the Oriental a few yards away. Of the fairly numer-

ous occupants of the Grand who managed to get out in time, one was a lady named Mrs. Morris Chichester-Smith, noted for the regal presence imparted by her height, which was almost six feet. At the moment of the shock, she was in a bathtub on the second floor. Supported by the interior piping, this convenience descended even more gradually than the rest of the structure, coming to rest finally in the middle of the wide street along the waterfront with Mrs. Chichester-Smith and most of her bath water still in it. A gallant witness of this remarkable scene had the aplomb to remove his own shirt and trousers and hand them to Mrs. Chichester-Smith, who put them on and proceeded to the waterfront. There a short time later she was forced to immerse herself again to escape the heat of the burning city.

In sharp contrast to the experience of Mrs. Chichester-Smith was that of her husband, who was possibly the only person in the Kanto area who experienced the great earthquake without being aware of it at all. Major Morris Chichester-Smith, who had been a well-known British ace during the war, was in Japan as a flying instructor to the Japanese Army. Like his wife, he had been making preprandial ablutions at the moment of the shock, but in his case the locale was the washroom of a train running between Yokohama and Kamakura. The motion of the train combined with the fact that his attention was engaged by a recalcitrant faucet prevented him from noticing anything unusual. Unlike many others in the region, his train was not derailed by the shock, and the engineer brought it quickly to a safe if somewhat bumpy stop. The Major then emerged from the washroom, asked what was wrong and was informed by his fellow passengers.

YOKOHAMA HAD ALREADY started to crash into ruins by the time the main shock reached Tokyo, some three seconds later. There, at the Imperial Hotel, the staff meeting in the office of Manager Tetsuzo Inumaru was still in progress. His recollections of what happened thereafter, later published in pamphlet form, provide a vivid picture of the scene:

When the building began to shake, I thought, "How about the kitchen?"—and started for those premises. On the way I saw the guests in the court and told them to just stay there; that was the safest place. When I got down to the kitchen, I found the electric ranges fallen over and all aflame, because some fat was on the stoves and fell over. Fire was coming out in every direction.

When I saw that fire in the kitchen, I looked around: "Is there anybody to help put out the fire?" Over in the corner there were four men under the table. "Can't you put the fire out?" I said. All the electricity was on. "Better turn off the main switch," I thought. I sent a boy to the power station. . . .

We put out the fire. The kitchen ceiling is very high and had not caught fire. In another ten minutes, the ranges would have been ruined and the walls have taken fire. . . .

Tetsuzo Inumaru's prompt action in the kitchen was one of the things that prevented fire in the Imperial from spreading. Another was some equally prompt action on the part of a young electrician by the name of Denji Morita who had joined the hotel staff on his graduation from engineering college two years before. Whether the messenger dispatched by Inumaru ever reached the power station is not recorded but it made little difference because Morita was already there. He had been in the power control room when the earthquake started, conducting a routine check of the gauges.

The possibility of faulty wiring is a notorious fire hazard in any new building. This was especially true in 1923 of a large new building in Japan where the use of electricity for cooking and heating was still a complete novelty. At the Imperial, a short circuit had already caused one serious fire which had destroyed the old wooden "annex," a remnant of the original hotel, the summer before. Better than anyone else on the staff, Morita understood what the consequences would be now if power continued to be supplied all over the building after an earthquake severe enough to have damaged most of the connections. In the circumstances, it would have been understandable enough if Morita had left the subterranean power room as fast as possible. Instead, he resolutely staggered across five yards of heaving floor and pulled down the main switch, thus shutting off the current throughout the structure by about the time that Inumaru was passing the courtyard gardens.

The Imperial Hotel stands close to the line between the marshy downtown area of Tokyo and the upland residential area to the west of it. Elsewhere in the city, the earthquake had widely varying effects depending largely upon location. On the rock-based hills to the west, many of the residents thought that the shock, while severe, was no worse than the semi-destructive one that had occurred the year before. Downtown, where the swampy filled-in ground provided better conduction for the surface waves, the effect was greatly intensified. While not as devastating as in Kamakura and points west, the impact was severe enough to create considerable havoc of which the most spectacular single instance took place in Tokyo's Asakusa amusement district, Tokyo's equivalent of Coney Island, where the usual Saturday afternoon crowds had begun to gather. This was the collapse of the celebrated Twelve-Story Tower, the city's highest building and one of its major attractions for rural sightseers.

Perceptibly influenced in conception by the more celebrated Tower of Pisa, Tokyo's tower lacked the former's unique slant but had compensating fascinations of its own. One of these was the view of the city from the balcony at the top, which was reached by a spiral ramp instead of a staircase and to which tickets were sold by an aged couple who ran the concession. Another was the recreation available at ground level where ladies of the town purveyed at bargain rates the same commodities that were available in Yoshiwara, a half mile to the north.

When the earthquake struck, the Twelve-Story Tower for a few astonishing seconds perfected the imitation of its Pisan model as it teetered back and forth. Then, according to one observer, "it seemed to make a polite bow" and broke apart at the eighth floor. By good fortune, the direction of the bow caused the upper four floors to crash, not into the milling crowd which surrounded the base on three sides, but into a small pond which was adjacent to the fourth side. Thus only a few bystanders were crushed to death in the debris—along with the old couple who ran the concession and a score or so of their clients. Two stagehands from a nearby theater, who had gone up to the balcony to have their lunch, were somehow thrown clear of the wreckage and into the pond where they survived, unhurt.

The room in which Makiko Aoki was getting ready for her trip to Oiso was not far from Asakusa but on the other side of the Sumida River. It formed part of the second floor of a detached building in the family compound; Mr. Aoki had had this building put up especially for her and her sister, to give them each a private room of her own where they could do their homework undisturbed by their noisy younger brothers. Makiko's room contained two pieces of real Western furniture, a chair and a desk. To Makiko, this room and its furniture—like her new laced shoes and the recently granted privilege of having an allowance of her own instead of having everything bought for her—were real signs of growing up; she was delighted with the whole arrangement. Now, when the first big shock rattled the walls and made the house sway more dangerously by far than any other quake in her remembrance, she still knew exactly what to do. First she crouched under the Western desk—so handy in an emergency—until the worst of the shock had passed. Then she got up, and putting the Western chair over her head—everyone knew that a Western chair over your head provided good protection in a really bad earthquake —she left her detached house and ran across the compound to the main one where her grandmother was cooking lunch.

70

In the main house she found not only her grandmother but her grandfather, uncle, and brother assembled for this meal, which had been scheduled a little earlier than usual. Her grandmother was the calmest of the group and seemed to be taking the attitude that no mere earthquake could throw her off her stride. "Let's all sit down and have our lunch," the old lady suggested; and while the house was being shaken intermittently by the aftershocks, the group actually took their places on the tatami around the low oblong table. However, they had not been there very long before Makiko's uncle decided to go up to the laundry-drying platform on the roof to have a look around.

When the uncle came down, he said that he had seen what appeared to be several fires starting up toward the south. Everyone else then went to have a look; and it was clear at once that he was entirely right. Half a dozen long thin fingers of smoke could now easily be seen, pointing straight up at the sky.

A half mile or so away in the same densely populated Honjo district, Dr. Ikeguchi—having carefully bandaged his patient's injured foot—was washing his hands in the basin at the corner of his office when the quake started. The main shock was violent enough to have knocked him off his feet if he had not been able to grasp the bowl with both hands to steady himself. When the shock began to subside, he went into the living room—where there had been no damage except to one glass electric-light shade which had fallen from the ceiling and smashed on the floor—and called all the members of his household together.

The household consisted of his wife, their nine-year-old daughter, two sons of five and three, and four servants. The latter were a nurse, a maid, a houseboy, and a rickshaw man to take the doctor on his sick-calls. Having assembled them, the doctor stated that it would be best, in view of the severity of the quake and the possibility of fire, for them all to take refuge elsewhere. Perhaps mindful of his last patient, he said that they should wear tabi—heavy foot coverings, shaped like leather stockings with a separate section for the big toe—since the streets would be full of broken tiles. He instructed his wife to distribute all the tabi that could be found in the house to the various members of the group, and to make sure the children put theirs on. He asked the maid to cook enough rice balls for everyone to eat during the afternoon, instead of lunch, and to slice plenty of pickled radish to go with them. Then, as they dispersed to follow these directions, he went out into the street to see what was happening. A rice-cracker shop at the corner of his street was already on fire, the smoke rising straight up into the hot still air. The shop had been deserted and no one was making the slightest effort to extinguish the flames.

CHAPTER IV

EDO NO HANA

THE FLOWERS OF EDO

THE TIME at which the Great Kanto Earthquake occurred —a few seconds less than two minutes before noon—had a special significance. It was the moment when fires had just been lighted in millions of kitchens all over the area, not only in the big hotels like the Imperial but in hundreds of smaller restaurants, thousands of urban lunch counters, tens of thousands of little wooden houses. This circumstance—combined with the construction of the houses and the special plan of the urban communities—meant that great conflagrations were sure to take place in almost every city affected by the quake. Tokyo's fire was inevitably the most extensive; the columns of smoke observed by Dr. Ikeguchi and Makiko Aoki were in fact the start of what was to become quite certainly the most horrifying conflagration that has ever occurred anywhere. However, the great fires in Tokyo had an immense area to cover and tremendous quantities of fuel to consume. It would be several hours before they reached their peak. Meanwhile, in the smaller cities to the southwest, where the quake had been even more violent, the fires got started much more rapidly.

73

While the fires sprang up more quickly in the smaller towns, there were also certain circumstances which tended to mitigate their effects, even in those communities where, unlike Ito, Atami and Kamakura, tsunami had helped to quench the flames. This was that, in the smaller towns, most of the inhabitants—excepting those who had been trapped in the ruins—had had a chance to escape into the surrounding countryside. Thus even in Odawara— which was wholly in flames within an hour and which burned to the ground that night—the loss of human life was proportionately much less than it was in Tokyo and Yokohama. At the great naval base of Yokosuka—a town of some 60,000—the lethal effects of an equally consuming fire were similarly curtailed. Here, in the first moment of the quake, 200 school children on an excursion train had been buried alive in the collapse of a high embankment beside the railroad station; at the same moment, oil storage tanks containing two years' supply of fuel for the entire fleet cracked and caught fire, causing a flow of burning oil into the harbor where it spread out in sheets of flame. Nonetheless, ships in the harbor as well as the surrounding countryside provided a refuge of sorts; the town burned to the ground, but the final death toll was the relatively modest one of some 700.

In Yokohama, as in Yokosuka, huge quantities of oil were stored; and the tanks of the Rising Sun and Standard Oil Companies were on high ground near the railroad station. When these tanks burst with the quake, oil ran down through the drainage canals and the Ooka River to the harbor, catching fire on the way. Not surprisingly, under these conditions, the conflagration in Yokohama —strung out along the waterfront in such a way as to offer maximum access to the freshening south wind—reached its peak while Tokyo's was still in its preliminary phases. Though not nearly so big as Tokyo's on an absolute scale, Yokohama's conflagration was proportionately even more destructive: 80 per cent of the city, instead of 60 per cent as in Tokyo, was eventually destroyed, and the count of known dead and missing reached 33,000 as compared to Tokyo's 107,000.

In Tokyo, the foreign community lived on the high ground west of the city, which was relatively immune to the fire as well as to the quake; so far as is known, not a single European died from either cause in the capital. In Yokohama, on the contrary, the foreign community suffered losses which were proportionately just as severe as those of the Japanese, if not more so. One of the most remarkable of these—which totaled some 250—was that of the young United States Consul, Max David Kirjassof, a naturalized citizen of Russian parentage, whose charred body was later found with those of his pregnant wife and their small daughter, in the garden of the consular residence. Away from home at the moment of the quake, Kirjassof had run back to rescue his family; all three had then been trapped by the flames before they could get away.

Deaths of United States citizens in foreign cities are recorded, each on a separate page, by all United States consulates in a Miscellaneous Record Book. The Yokohama Miscellaneous Record Book, in which Kirjassof's death was briefly summarized by his successor, contains thirty-eight pages devoted to other United States victims of the quake. Among them was Miss Jennie Cuyper, principal of the Ferris Girls' Seminary, who had come back from Karuizawa only the night before to get the school ready for the start of the autumn term on the following Monday. Pinned under the burning wreckage of the school building, from which other members of the faculty and some students who happened to be on hand were trying to rescue her, she realized that the fire must reach her before they could get her out. Her last words, her rescuers reported later, were, "I am being summoned by my Heavenly Father. Go now. The fire is close." When the flames began to catch their clothes, they were obliged to follow her instructions. From the nearby garden, they heard her cry, "Goodbye, all," and start to sing a hymn.

In the downtown business section of Yokohama, most of those

75

who had not been killed in the quake or trapped in the wreckage tried to take refuge in one of three ways. The most obvious—and, as it proved eventually, the safest, despite the patches of burning oil—was the waterfront. Here with the fire at their backs, the refugees could gain some protection from the flames by standing waist-deep or neck-deep along the beach. Thousands did so all through the first night, surviving until small boats came to take them to safety on the larger ships that were anchored or moored in the harbor.

Many others in the crowded section of town, finding themselves blocked away from the shore by fire, sought safety in the canals or the river. In these waterways, burning oil and burning sampans, drifting downstream after fire had severed their mooring ropes, were not the only hazard. Yokohama—along with the other cities on Tokyo Bay—experienced no tsunami like those on the shore of Sagami Bay, but the water level dropped two or three feet shortly after the quake and remained lower than usual for several hours thereafter. As the water level of the bay fell, it drew the water out of the canals as well, so that these fell to half, or less than half, of their average normal depth of four feet or so. With flames pressing in from both sides, this was often less than enough to provide protection; and of those persons who took refuge in the canals, thousands died by fire. One of the fortunate ones who survived was Tsuneyuki Isono, a young businessman who, with his wife, sought safety in the Ooka River upstream from the oil tanks. When the flames subsided, they crawled out of the water onto a bridge the surface of which remained strangely but agreeably warm all through the night. In the morning Isono crawled down the bank to find out why. He found that the bridge was being heated like a stove by a smoldering barge that had run aground underneath it.

A third possible refuge for downtown Yokohama was Yokohama Park, an area of some twenty acres, a mile or so in from the shore.

Into it swarmed many thousands who were shut off by walls of fire from the waterfront. Broken water mains that had made it impossible from the start for the fire department to combat the flames were here a blessing in disguise. Leakage turned the park into a swamp, and the moisture helped those in the center of the area—unlike thousands on the perimeter who burned to death— to stand the heat of the fire that pressed in from all four sides.

Among those who reached Yokohama Park and survived there was a young financial reporter named Kuniharu Namikata. Making the rounds of the silk companies to get news when the quake struck, he had been trapped in the collapse of a wooden building, unhurt but pinned down by a heavy beam. He shouted for help and for a time heard rescuers working toward him with shouts of promise and encouragement. Abruptly, all these noises ceased and were replaced by an ominous silence. Realizing that his rescuers had fled and that this could only mean the approach of fire, Namikata made a superhuman effort to free himself, somehow managed to do so, and wriggled out onto a smoky and deserted street. He ran to the corner, turned it, and there almost bumped into the head of the Silk Exchange who caused him wry amusement, even under these dire circumstances, by saying, "Your paper should be proud of you for risking your life this way to get the story of the fire!"

Together, the two men found their way through the burning streets to the park. They spent the night there, plastering themselves with mud as protection against the heat.

To many of those who could find no way through the flames either to the waterfront or to the park, the safest refuge seemed to be the Yokohama Specie Bank, a supposedly fireproof stone building which was one of the half-dozen or so such structures that had remained standing after the quake. Here the employees of the bank, and later several hundred others, took refuge in the basement vaults. Eventually, the doors had to be closed and hundreds of outsiders who came too late burned to death while trying to get in. As it turned out, these outsiders were the lucky ones. Fire eventually found its way into the building through window frames bent by the shock. The hundreds in the cellar died a more lingering death, by slow heat and suffocation.

Even the calamity of the Yokohama Specie Bank was perhaps less dreadful than the one which was witnessed that night by Dante Dentici and his father. On their way to the waterfront, they had been intercepted by a wall of fire and had taken refuge in a swamp below a steep cliff at one end of the Bluff. That night, hundreds of residents of the Bluff were cornered by the flames on the edge of this cliff, where they apparently had the choice of burning to death or risking a hundred-foot fall. When they were forced to jump, those who did so landed on top of those who had jumped before and were too badly injured to crawl out of the way. Dante Dentici listened to the screams of the injured and dying all through the night; by daylight it was discovered that there was an obscure footpath down the side of the cliff by which many might have found their way to safety.

In the year 1861, the Japanese government sent an official mission around the world to see how other nations lived and then report on the subject. The diary of this mission makes fascinating reading, but to Europeans the amount of space given by its authors to the methods of fire prevention employed in Western countries may seem strangely disproportionate. To readers in Japan, for whom the report was compiled, the emphasis on this topic seems appropriate enough.

While it is true that major earthquakes in Japan almost always cause major conflagrations, it by no means follows that earthquakes are the only agents of such calamities. On the contrary, all Japanese cities, and most of all the largest, have always been acutely susceptible to fire from any cause whatever. During the two and a half centuries of the Tokugawa shogunate, during which Edo had between one and two million inhabitants, well over 500 major fires were recorded. Of these, each of over 100 consumed more than 3,000 houses; no fewer than 50 were greater in area, and far more destructive of human life, than the Great Fire of London in 1666, which was the Western world's worst conflagration in the corresponding period.

During the Tokugawa era, the capital lacked not only water mains but fire-fighting apparatus of any sort except buckets and house-wrecking utensils. Under these conditions, the only chance of stopping a fire was at the very start. Once a whole house was in flames, others were sure to catch too; the procedure favored in such cases was simply to try to keep the conflagration as narrow as possible while letting it advance with the wind until it reached a wide vacant space or the edge of town—or until there was rain. Most of the greatest Edo fires, like that of 1772 which took 25,000 lives, traced a long thin trail across the city. There were, however, exceptions when great fires escaped from even this limited form of control. Greatest of all the Edo fires was that of 1657, which, assisted by a strong northwest wind, spread out like a fan across 6,000 acres of the downtown part of the city and caused almost 100,000 deaths before it burned out at last on the shores of the bay.

Great fires were part of Edo routine; the saying went that no life span was complete unless it included three of them. Endurance of the suffering they caused became part of the fierce, proud samurai tradition of a capital which made Sparta seem sybaritic by comparison. The true "Edokko"—a resident whose forbears had lived in the capital for at least three generations—scorned all such catastrophes just as he scorned to heat his house in winter, and all the more if the house chanced to be a castle. Edo had a stoic proverb: *"Nana-korobi, ya-oki,"* "fall down seven times, get

79

up eight," which put the viewpoint in a terse nutshell. A man who lost everything in a fire and then rebuilt his fortunes was entitled to special status and respect. The eloquent urban slang term for the great fires—*Edo no hana,* the Flowers of Edo—was not, a sarcastic slur but the expression of a bitter, sophisticated pride.

During the Meiji era, aided by information brought back by the round-the-world mission, Tokyo had somewhat modified its traditional attitude. A competent metropolitan fire department had been organized where nine hundred permanent members and fourteen hundred auxiliaries were disposed at thirty stations strategically scattered through the city. It was these dedicated firemen who had pruned the Flowers of Edo so effectively that, in the sixty years since the Restoration, there had been only ten conflagrations of 3,000-house dimensions.

In Tokyo as elsewhere, the complete breakdown of telephone communication immediately after the Kanto earthquake prevented the reporting of most of the individual fires that started either then or later. Nonetheless, according to later estimates, 136 were spotted by the fire department during the first hour and of these 36 were actually extinguished. However, the gentle breeze that had been almost imperceptible at noon increased just enough to provide a favorable draft for the remaining ones, through doors and windows left open to the summer air. As the sparks and flakes of fire rose with the heat of the flames and floated on the breeze, the fact that the quake had shaken the tiles off many roofs assumed major significance. This exposed the wooden footings of the roofs to the blowing contagion and made tinder of many buildings that might otherwise have remained reasonably fireproof. The fires traveled, joined and multiplied with predictable rapidity.

Immediately after the first shock, the chief of Tokyo's fire department perceived that he was confronted with an emergency of unprecedented size and sort. From the department's central observation tower, fires could be seen springing up all over town. Equally alarming soon afterward was the confusion in the streets caused by people—most of them pulling household belongings along with them on handcarts—trying to find their way through the maze of fires toward some place of safety. There was no way for headquarters to communicate with local stations except by individual messengers on foot. Messengers were sent to the stations to tell each one to act on its own initiative.

While the good work of the fire department helped to save the central part of the city and, later on, part of the university section, the fires in the downtown districts made rapid headway. Not one but several conflagrations developed on each side of the Sumida. The one on the right, or west, bank of the river got its multiple start in the Asakusa district, where the small lunch counters, scattered about through the amusement park, caught fire immediately and were deserted by their proprietors as soon as they found it impossible to extinguish the flames. A few blocks away, the Yoshiwara quarter was also blazing in half a dozen places. On the left side of the river, in the Honjo district, the fires were a little slower in starting but they covered an even wider area. As these two separate and complex conflagrations acquired shape and direction, an interesting tactical development occurred. On each side of the Sumida, people who were threatened by the flames or who saw that they soon might be, reasoned that if they could only get across the river all would be well. Thus on each side of the river there was a huge swarm of desperately frightened people, most of them with highly inflammable household goods piled on handcarts, hurrying toward the bridges, and toward each other, neither swarm realizing that the other side of the river was also in flames.

In the last three miles of its course toward the muddy waters of Tokyo Bay, the Sumida, in 1923 as it is now, was crossed by five bridges at intervals of half a mile or so. Normally these bridges—which in 1923 were constructed entirely of wood—were quite ample to accommodate the flow of traffic, most of it pedestrian. On the afternoon of September 1, understandably enough, they proved to be inadequate for the conflicting tides. The advance groups of refugees from each side perceived as they reached the bridges that there was no sense crossing them—but by then the pressure of those behind made it impossible to turn back. Some of the refugees were momentarily reassured by the thought that the bridge itself, which would be somewhat removed from the flames on either side, might be a safe place to stay. Later refugees, however, naturally had the same thought and they too pushed toward the center.

As the fire closed in on the river from both sides, and as more newcomers pushed onto the bridges, those who were at or near the center jumped, or were pushed, into the water. Those who could swim were less fortunate than those who could not; the latter drowned quickly whereas the former, in most cases, were gradually burned to death. So, eventually, were those who remained on the bridges. Sparks and flakes of flame fell onto the inflammable piles of belongings the refugees had brought with them. First these caught fire and then the bridges themselves. Of the five, only one, the Shin-Ohashi, remained standing the next day. Its survival was due primarily to the courage and good sense of a policeman named Gensaku Hatori, who saw that the prime fire hazards were the handcarts, bundles of bedding and other paraphernalia which the refugees had brought with them. He and his subordinates allowed no one carrying anything to step on the Shin-Ohashi bridge—thus saving the lives of some 12,000 people who used it as a refuge.

The rush of refugees toward the bridges was only one of many mass migrations within Tokyo. In fact, the whole city, or at least the downtown part of it, was on the move, often apparently in all directions at the same time. In some respects, the situation was comparable to that of a forest fire in which animals are flushed by the flames and driven ahead of them, but there was one significant difference. Forest fires almost invariably have only a single point of origin and develop as a single front of flame, proceeding in a predictable direction. In this case, the fire had many separate origins and it was proceeding every which way. Those who were fleeing did so in conflicting streams which collided with each other and made impassable traffic jams—of which those on the bridges were by no means the only ones never to be untangled.

In the downtown district of Tokyo, there were three large vacant areas which formed the most logical places of refuge and toward which most of the refugees eventually headed. One was the great open space of some two square miles in front of the Imperial Palace known as the Imperial Palace Plaza. Lying between the downtown section and the hilly residential district to the west, and ordinarily used for parades, demonstrations and Sunday strolling, this served to accommodate many thousands of refugees from the crowded Ginza and Kanda districts, bordering it on the east and north, who were lucky enough to reach it.

For residents of the downtown Asakusa district, on the right, or west bank of the Sumida, the most likely refuge was Ueno Park, the city's most spacious, and the site of its zoo and its largest art museum. Tens of thousands of refugees reached Ueno Park and survived safely. So did all the zoo animals—unlike those of the smaller private menagerie in the Asakusa amusement park.

For citizens who lived on the east side of the river in the Honjo and Fukagawa areas, the best and indeed the only refuge was the Army Clothing Depot, as the vacant area was still called by the inhabitants of the district. Taken together with the adjoining Yasuda residence gardens—although these were walled in and not accessible to the general public—this formed a space totaling perhaps twenty-five acres; and the width of the river itself, on which the gardens fronted, broadened the noninflammable space to almost twice that. Using the discretionary powers granted them by the Metropolitan Chief, the fire stations and the police passed the

83

word through the Honjo district that residents should head for the Clothing Depot. By one o'clock—at which time thick columns of smoke were visible all over the area—refugees had begun to arrive at the Depot in considerable numbers.

It was during the next four or five hours that the fire in Tokyo developed steadily into what became, eventually, without any doubt, the greatest single conflagration ever ignited on the surface of the globe. Comparable fires were started in Japan during World War II—not only the atom-bomb fires at Hiroshima and Nagasaki but also those resulting from the vast incendiary raids at Tokyo on March 10, and at Yokohama on May 29, of 1945. None of these, however, exceeded the Tokyo earthquake fire in destructive effect or came close to it in area.

It should not be supposed, however, that anything like the whole of Tokyo was burning. On the contrary, due in part to the efforts of the fire department and in part to accidents of meteorology and the city plan, the upland residential area remained largely unscathed, except for a few relatively small and independent fires. Some residents of the elevated parts of town had what amounted to a grandstand view of the proceedings, and many witnesses recall the scene as one of dreadful but undeniable beauty. Due to the effect of the intense sudden heat from below upon the cooler air above, a huge and marvelously fluffy white cloud was formed above the city, making a magnificent contrast with the black and smoky atmosphere closer to the ground. The flames themselves sparkled in red ripples and waves, like a fiery sea, stretching across the whole lower part of town along a horizon of several miles. On a much grander scale, it was like looking into the inside of a furnace. As it grew darker, the flames towered higher into the air—impossible to see how far, but as dusk fell, the impression was created that the sky itself was on fire. Actually, meteorologists later estimated that the flames themselves—as distinct from their reflection on the clouds—probably reached a height of not more than three hundred feet, although large patches of flimsy burning material were swept by the immense upward draft as high as five miles.

Watching the fire from the uplands as it developed through the afternoon, observers found it hard to believe that there were actually people moving around under what looked like a solid sea of flame. Actually, of course, there were many thousands—most of them by no means very sharply aware of their peril. Among them were the methodical Dr. Ikeguchi and Makiko Aoki, in her new dress and her new laced shoes.

In Makiko Aoki's case, what had happened was that, after joining her father and his twenty-five workmen in the spectacle-frame factory, a conference had been held to determine the best course of action. While the conference was going on, one of the workmen had gone out into the street to reconnoiter the situation and had come back to report that the police were suggesting that everyone take refuge in the Clothing Depot. Mr. Aoki thought this a good plan and recommended that both the members of his family and his workmen follow it. Since Makiko already had her overnight things packed up in her beach towel in preparation for the weekend at Oiso, there was no reason for her to delay. She could set out with four of the workmen immediately; her grandmother and her small brother could come along later. Mr. Aoki and the remaining employees would try to put things in order at the factory and then join the others. Makiko was to wait for her grandmother near the entrance, so that the family could remain united.

Once she was out in the street, Makiko saw that, in going to the Depot, she could not take the route through the small streets and narrow alleys that led there most directly. They were littered with

85

tiles and debris that would have made walking very difficult, if not impossible; it would be better to go by the wider main street where the trolley tracks ran.

On reaching this main street, she saw two or three stalled trolleys deserted by their passengers but not by their conductors and motormen who stood anxiously beside them. The street was crowded and most of the other people seemed, like herself, to be headed toward the Depot in the understanding that this was where the police wanted them to go. As the jam grew worse and walking slower, one of the workmen suggested to Makiko that it might be better to cross one of the bridges and head for Ueno Park. Makiko considered this suggestion but rejected it; her father had told her to go to the Depot and if she went elsewhere, her grandmother would miss her, and considerable worry and confusion might result.

The walk to the Depot, which would normally have been a matter of ten minutes or so, this time took an hour. When she got there, Makiko saw at once that the crowd was so big that her grandmother would have difficulty finding her. Her beach towel had a distinctive pattern on it that any member of her family would be sure to recognize. She found a long stick, tied the towel to it, and, holding the stick so that the towel was well above her head, took up a position near the entrance to the Depot.

As for Dr. Ikeguchi, his original plan had been to leave the house with his family as soon as they had completed their preparations. This proved impractical because, before they could all get started, people who had been injured in the first shock began to appear at the clinic for treatment. Toward two o'clock, two porters from the Yasuda house turned up with a handcart; they said that, as there was danger of the fire's spreading, they had been instructed to come and help the doctor load his household effects and to bring them, along with his family, to refuge at the residence. Dr. Ikeguchi went on attending to his new group of patients while

86

his wife and the servants loaded the cart. When they were ready to leave, he told them to go ahead; he would join them when he could get away. They were to wait for him beside the Western-style house near the gate of the Yasuda compound on the side nearest the river.

The conscientious doctor stayed on in his clinic until well after three o'clock. By that time, the house was within hearing distance of the flames, and a strong breeze from the south was blowing the fire toward it. When at last the doctor set out, he had to dodge flames as he hurried along through the littered streets. However, when he reached the Yasuda compound, the fire was well behind him and he found his family and the servants without difficulty.

The Yasudas' Western-style house, to the left of the gate, was the first brick residence that had been built in Tokyo and a landmark in the neighborhood. Mrs. Ikeguchi and the others were standing exactly where the doctor had told them to wait. Mrs. Ikeguchi, seeing that the smoke clouds were becoming darker and closer, had begun to be worried about his getting there; when he finally arrived, she and the children made it plain that they were very glad to see him. Just then the Yasudas' butler came out of the house and urged them all to come in and have tea. The doctor thanked him but said no, they would stay in the garden.

By now it was getting on toward four o'clock and the doctor noticed that the wind was becoming gradually stronger and less steady in direction; from time to time, but with increasing frequency, it blew sparks and flakes of fire all the way across the river. The scene was disturbing, for obviously the fire on the other side of the Sumida was completely out of hand—but still there certainly seemed to be no immediate danger. The rickshaw man said that he, for one, was hungry and the doctor suddenly realized that none of them had had their lunch. The maid and Mrs. Ikeguchi unpacked the rice balls and passed them around, and the group began to eat. The children seemed to be enjoying themselves; it was rather

like a new sort of family picnic. When some other children nearby
—for there were by this time perhaps a dozen other families, fifty
or sixty people in all, taking refuge in the compound—indicated
that they were hungry too, the Ikeguchis invited them to come
over and share whatever there was.

Very suddenly, as they were all sitting in the garden eating this
improvised lunch, an extraordinary sound, like that of some huge
airplane flying close to the ground, became audible—first in the
distance, then closer, then right at hand. At the same time, the sky
grew much darker, almost black. Dr. Ikeguchi's five-year-old son,
about to pop a second rice ball into his mouth, stopped his hand
on the way. He stood with his mouth wide open, staring bewildered
at the night-dark sky.

CHAPTER V

TATSUMAKI

DRAGON TWISTS

ACCORDING TO THE RESEARCHES of the distinguished Professor Akitsune Imamura, loss of human life in direct consequence of a major earthquake where no fire is involved is unlikely to exceed one person for every eleven houses destroyed. Since not more than 10,000 houses in Tokyo were demolished by the quake, this ratio would have resulted in fewer than 1,000 deaths for the capital. Had the same average applied elsewhere, the total loss of life would not have been much more than 8,000 or 9,000.

That, instead, the death count reached some 140,000—if, as seems logical, the missing are included—was due to the fires, but here too special causes were at work, particularly in Tokyo. One of these causes was the network of bridges that cross not only the Sumida River but the city's numerous drainage canals. Of a total of some 350 bridges in the burned area, more than 250 were destroyed—in many cases for the very reason that they were being used as refuges by people who brought with them large quantities of highly inflammable household goods. But the magnitude of the death toll was attributable less to these many mass catastrophes than one other special factor. This was a change in the weather that occurred during the fire and in large part because of it.

The same updraft that had caused the picturesque cumulus clouds noted by the spectators watching the fire from the hills west of Tokyo also caused a partial vacuum near the ground. As the surrounding air rushed in to fill it, the breeze freshened in Tokyo; in the harbor at Yokohama, the wind became almost a gale. The anonymous observer on the *Philoctetes* continued to have a splendid vantage point from which to observe the scene, and he described it vividly:

Fires ashore assumed huge proportions, fanned by the southerly gale. Sampans and large cargo lighters, now unattended on account of the rough seas and in many instances because of more important rescue work ashore which the boatmen had to perform, took fire, broke from their moorings and were carried by the wind and sea across the harbour. There were many of these boat-furnaces travelling rapidly, burning fiercely, making straight for the ships at anchor. Most of these lighters were laden with logs, planks and "baby squares" recently discharged from American and Canadian cargo holds and, once ablaze, could hardly be extinguished in that gale. On they came, right in the path of the ocean-going vessels.

The hazard caused by the burning sampans, combined with the wind and the oil fires, led to further difficulties. The *London Maru,* having left her mooring close inshore to get farther away from the fire, was caught by the wind and swung against the Blue Funnel liner *Lycaon.* In getting clear, she then smashed up against first the *Philoctetes* and then back again into the *Lycaon* before finally getting off and mooring to another Japanese freighter. Meanwhile, the *Philoctetes's* captain—noted for his exploits in dodging submarines during the war—maneuvered his ship skillfully past the collisions, through the smashed breakwater and into the open harbor. By five o'clock, a dozen large ships had followed her outside the breakwater, and at 5:15 the *Philoctetes* weighed anchor and set a course for Kobe. As she rounded the Miura Peninsula and headed down the coast, her passengers saw the two huge beacons of the Yokosuka oil tanks—which went on burning for a month—and later, as darkness fell, the bright embers of the towns and villages along the shore of Sagami Bay.

As the *Philoctetes* steamed southwest along the coast, another liner, the *West Prospect*, passed her inward bound. En route from the United States to Kobe via Manila, she had run short of fresh water and was putting in at Yokohama to take some aboard. Her first intimation of what was happening on shore was the astonishing glow made by the burning city against the night sky. Fresh water was the last thing available at Yokohama. The next morning, the *West Prospect* went on her way again, after leaving some food and medical supplies and taking aboard some fifteen passengers, who, on September 3, were among the first of several hundred refugees from Yokohama eventually brought by ship to Kobe.

On shore, the acceleration of the wind that had created the commotion in the harbor had even more noteworthy consequences. It enabled the fires in both Tokyo and Yokohama to multiply their momentum, just as the draft in a fireplace becomes stronger and more effective as the fire becomes hotter. In Yokohama the fires had started too fast and spread too far for the fire department to be able to make any serious efforts at containment, but in Tokyo the chief of the fire department, perceiving from his observation tower that the individual stations could do nothing more on their own initiative, adopted a new plan. This was for them to combine efforts and concentrate on confining the major conflagration to the downtown area.

At 4:30, the local chiefs, summoned to headquarters by messengers, were instructed to take action toward this end. Consisting largely of systematic demolition, which was assisted by the Army Engineering Corps and also by a shift in the wind during the evening from south through west to north, the effort was reasonably successful. It cost the lives of twenty members of the department but led eventually to the third stage of the fight against the fire in which it was eventually subdued, in the early morning hours of September 3. By the time the second stage began, however, the downtown conflagration, which eventually covered an area of some 10,000 acres, had reached proportions which also created certain special meteorological conditions of its own. Just as the earthquake had triggered the fire, the great fire now triggered a series of whirlwinds and tornadoes. It was these freak fiery storms, and most especially the tornadoes, that gave the earthquake conflagration its special character and its appalling climax.

In speaking of whirlwinds and tornadoes, it is necessary to make a technical distinction between the two. Whirlwinds, which are most commonly exemplified by the swirl of dust at a street corner, are comparatively simple phenomena, likely to occur when any two currents of air, such as those that may be created when wind is divided by a block of houses, suddenly meet and mingle. During a great conflagration, which pulls drafts through streets that serve as chimneys, such whirlwinds are frequent and have special characteristics. One is that as the air mingles with the fire and grows hot, it tends to spin upward, carrying sparks, patches of flame and light pieces of burning material, thus spreading the fire further.

Quite distinct from the simple mechanism of the ordinary whirlwind is the complex one of the tornado. Well known in the United States Southwest as "twisters," and in other parts of the world by similar picturesque nicknames, tornadoes belong to the family of great revolving windstorms that also includes cyclones, hurricanes and typhoons. Unlike whirlwinds, which originate near the surface of the ground, tornadoes originate from the turbulence within clouds and consist essentially of a deflection of that turbulence toward the ground. Like the other revolving windstorms, tornadoes always spin counterclockwise in the Northern hemisphere and clockwise in the Southern, owing to the effect upon them of the earth's rotation. Tornadoes are the smallest of the great circular storms but by no means necessarily the least violent. They are far more powerful than whirlwinds and spin at greater speeds which often exceed 100 miles an hour.

The rich, fluffy cumulus cloud caused by the Tokyo fire—although many people in the crowd at the Depot and elsewhere mistook it for the sign of a coming thunder shower, which might extinguish the flames—contained no rain whatsoever. It did, however, contain strong interior turbulence, which, in complex response to the violent updraft, deflected not one but numerous tornadoes into the area of the conflagration. Despite the characteristic of having been deflected downward from a cloud, the "spin" of a tornado has an upward tilt which may be very strong; "twisters" often tip over cars, tear off roofs and destroy barns or houses. The tornadoes that developed in both Tokyo and Yokohama on the afternoon of the Two Hundred and Tenth Day were not especially powerful when compared to the most destructive ones recorded in the United States Southwest. Nonetheless, they were far more lethal than these for the simple reason that in most cases they were, in effect, made out of fire.

Under the conditions of the Tokyo conflagration, both whirlwinds and tornadoes presented much the same appearance—a murky column of black smoke laced with flame—and, though not many survivors could report on this detail, both made much the same kind of noise. They shared one other common characteristic. Fire of any sort uses up oxygen and in its place creates poisonous carbon monoxide, of which a relatively small amount can cause death when inhaled. Oxygen is so plentiful that most of the time, even during a great conflagration, there is enough to sustain both the fire and the people—unless both are in the same place, in which case the people usually burn to death anyway. However, in the case of fiery whirlwinds or tornadoes, this may not hold true. In Tokyo, when a large whirlwind or tornado passed over an area it often left so much carbon monoxide in its wake that even those who had not been burned to death died within a very few minutes from the effects of the poison.

During the Tokyo earthquake-fire, whirlwinds occurred at street intersections or anywhere else that strong horizontal air currents from different directions met. True tornadoes developed mainly at fairly wide, open areas—apparently because these provided gaps in the general updraft of the fire as a whole. Observers were rarely in a position to distinguish one from the other; and since, like the English word "whirlwind," the more descriptive Japanese term "tatsumaki," or "dragon twist," can be loosely applied to either, it is not always possible to be sure from eyewitness accounts which was which. In Yokohama, for example, the official reports state that there were thirty whirlwinds between four and eight o'clock, seventeen of which were mobile and the biggest of which covered a total distance of 2,200 meters. The very precision of these figures—as is the case with much of the statistical information available about the whole disaster—renders them slightly suspect; in any event, while some of these whirlwinds were undoubtedly tornadoes, it is impossible to tell which ones.

Of the fifty or so tatsumaki recorded in Tokyo, it is extremely difficult, for understandable reasons, to obtain very satisfactory descriptions. The basic difficulty, caused by the scarcity of surviving witnesses, is compounded by the tendency of witnesses who did survive either to embroider their reminiscences or to draw erroneous conclusions. An interesting example of the latter was the report of a tornado in the Asakusa district by an observer who said that he had seen it draw a policeman through the door of the police barracks and then blow him out from a second-story window. This seems to have been illusion based on substitution, of the sort frequently practiced by magicians. What really happened, as determined by police records, was that there were two policemen involved; one ran into the building and the other jumped out the upstairs window to escape the flames.

Another story was told by a man who was borne off by a tatsumaki and dropped gently in the middle of Tokyo Bay, whence he eventually swam back safely to shore. This man has never been found. Other stories about the tatsumaki have a ring of truth; and in a good many cases, circumstantial evidence, chiefly the condition of the corpses, proved that the cause of death was carbon monoxide rather than roasting. A case in point was the tragedy that took place in an open space near the Yoshiwara district where 600 or so of its denizens were found dead the next day. Many of these had died by drowning in a pond where they had tried to take refuge, and others had been burned to death. Some of the corpses, however, were neither burned nor submerged. Their condition indicated that a tornado had also passed over the area.

Circumstantial evidence was especially plentiful in the case of the most violent of all the earthquake-fire tatsumaki, which was not only a genuine tornado but almost indisputably the most destructive one that ever occurred. This one developed over the lower reaches of the Sumida River a few minutes before four o'clock, veered to the west and then some fifteen minutes later crossed the river toward the east. The most expert description of its appearance and behavior was again that provided by Professor Imamura, writing in the Japanese periodical *Scientific Knowledge:*

It was 100 to 200 meters high and its width was about that of the Sumo Stadium. It swirled counterclockwise and swept off little barges two or four meters from the surface of the river. The smoke and flame of the School of Industry on the Asakusa side added to its strength. It then moved over to the opposite side, toward the Clothing Depot, swept past the middle of the Yasuda residence, and reached the Depot. The approximate velocity of the whirlwind must have been seventy to eighty meters a second.

While Professor Imamura's description is doubtless accurate, it does not purport to be more than a scientific record of the occurrence. For details of what the whirlwind looked and felt like it is more helpful to turn to the recollections of the few members of the crowd of forty thousand who both saw and survived it and to circumstantial evidence of its force. Such evidence includes heavy sheets of zinc bent around the branches of a tree, wrinkled bicycles festooning the branches of other trees, and a large horse cart deposited in the middle of one of the Yasuda fish ponds. Eyewitness accounts include that of a policeman from the nearby station who said:

I heard a terrible noise, like the sound of a waterfall. The water of the river by the Yasuda residence was swirling about fifteen meters into the air. A barge turned over; the waterspout headed toward the Yasuda residence and turned into a black pillar. It seemed to me that it swirled counterclockwise.

A sergeant from another police station nearby had somewhat similar recollections:

A half-constructed house was blown down. The sky grew dark. I was blown down flat on the ground. As I lay there gravel hit my face. Zinc roofing and scaffolding came flying by. I saw a man whose legs were broken by a flying log. An eighteen-year-old girl came along, rolling like a ball. . . .

The sergeant's reference to the zinc roofing and scaffolding is significant: by August the municipal government had started to prepare for the construction of an elementary school and several other buildings at one corner of the Depot, and much of the material and equipment to be used was collected there. This equipment included numerous telephone booths, which figure in several accounts of the whirlwind. A government official who was in the

96

crowd on the south side of the Depot recalled that at about four o'clock,

a strong wind accompanied by a deafening sound started blowing from the river. Open-mouthed, everyone stood stock still and uttered a deep sigh. . . . Although I had hidden my head under a cart, it was injured by the huge branch of a tree. I picked up the roof of a telephone booth, hid myself under it and held a piece of flannel over my nose and mouth. The wind made a whistling sound. . . .

Another anonymous survivor related similar experiences:

I went out in the street to borrow a few wooden sliding doors and straw mats to cover them up. My family, consisting of ten people, hid under carts or wooden doors. . . . A terrifying wind started blowing from the southwest and in an instant had carried away our wooden doors and straw mats. . . . The cart next to ours went high up in the sky and fell on the roof of the post office. As I looked in amazement, hundreds of people were taken into the air like so many beans. The first whirlwind lasted for about twenty minutes. About ten minutes after it had started, fire flakes began to fall like rain. Carts loaded with belongings as well as our clothes caught fire. There was a pool of water near me and I dipped my towel in it and kept my body from the heat. The whirlwind sounded like an airplane engine. People rushed to the center of the Depot. . . .

Across the river, on the west bank, the janitor of the School of Industry, who lived in a shed on the school grounds and who had found a safe refuge-nook on the riverbank, said that he had counted no less than ten whirlwinds during the course of the afternoon. Most of them were in the form of pillars of smoke which became fiery when they passed through a burning area. They were about as high as the tallest factory chimneys. Between four and five in the afternoon, he heard an indescribable sound coming from the direction of the Depot. Another observer reported seeing a tall slanting pillar of fire cross the river, toward the Yasuda residence. The observer who had the most complete impression of what happened there was Dr. Ikeguchi.

A FEW INSTANTS after Dr. Ikeguchi noticed the bewildered expression on the face of his small son as he stared at the black sky, things began to happen very rapidly at the Yasuda residence. Huge flames began to lash the trees. The strange roaring noise became deafeningly loud. There was a wind of indescribable force and heat.

Two policemen who were sitting on the cart containing the Ikeguchi belongings were blown away—one toward the entrance of the house, the other into the air and out of sight. A two-foot-thick pasania tree was twisted out of the ground and carried off toward the north. Other trees were twisted out of the ground or blown down flat against it. All this occurred in a second or two. Dr. Ikeguchi tried to shout to the other people in the compound, to tell them to go nearer to the gate. His voice was inaudible even to himself.

The doctor by this time had his five-year-old son on his back and was holding his daughter in his arms. The smaller boy was tied to his mother's back. Thinking to lead everyone into the river, the doctor motioned toward his wife that they should move toward the gate, but they could make no headway. His wife signaled that they should try to get around the corner of the house. They tried, succeeded and found themselves for a moment out of the worst of the wind. But in a moment they saw great red banners of flame snapping across the river toward the garden.

At the front door of the house, the driveway ran under an old-fashioned porte-cochere of which the entrance faced the river. This porte-cochere was so long as to be almost a tunnel and it seemed to the doctor that it might possibly offer some protection. Partly through their own efforts and partly pushed by the wind, his family, the servants and some people from other groups in the garden crowded into it. It was no use. Flames blew into one end and then through it. The tunnellike form of the porte-cochere made it a sort of trap; they could not go back because of the wind, and two cars, both now burning, blocked the other end. The flames which rushed through the tunnel were mixed with boiling spray, drawn from the river. Some of the group were praying, others screaming or moaning. Dr. Ikeguchi now realized that there was nothing for them all to do except stay where they were and wait for death.

A few minutes later the wind died down and he became aware that the screaming and moaning had stopped. Instead, there was total silence in the tunnel. He looked around at the others and at once knew why. They were all dead.

Dr. Ikeguchi arranged the bodies of his three children and his wife on the ground. He lay down beside them thinking that now he would die also. Instead of dying, he went on thinking; and the thought came to him that when he died there would be no one to bury the bodies of the others. He decided to try to live at least long enough to place their bodies in the care of someone whom he could trust. This objective became his chief concern. Finding it easier to breathe with his head close to the ground, he began to crawl out of the tunnel toward the gate near the river. The wind pushed him back but he went on trying, making his objective a pasania tree near the gate, which, he recalled, had loose earth near its roots. Finally he reached this tree and put his face in the soft earth so that he could breathe through it. Meanwhile, fire burned the backs of his hands to the bone. It burned all the hair and all the skin off the top of his head. It burned off both his ears. The black alpaca coat he was wearing gave protection to his back and for some reason did not burn away.

Still determined to reach the gate, and beyond it the river, Dr. Ikeguchi thought that perhaps he could do so by climbing over the wall instead of trying to reach the gate that led through it. He got to the wall, but the first time he tried to scramble over it the wind blew him back. He tried again and this time, whether through his own effort or because the plaster of the wall was so weakened by the fire that it crumbled under his weight, he crossed it. There was a road and, on the other side of it, the water. He jumped into it and heard the voice of someone he knew—a policeman from his block. The water relieved the pain of his burns, and Dr. Ikeguchi began to understand that he was not going to die.

The tornado that had crossed the river into the Yasuda garden, killing all the members of Dr. Ikeguchi's family, also killed almost everyone else there, including the occupants of the Western-style house, which burned to the ground. Its owner, Yoshio Yasuda, was found the next morning among the numerous corpses at the foot of the same pasania tree under which Dr. Ikeguchi had found it possible to breathe through the loose earth; he was still alive but died later in the day. In the Yasuda gardens, however, the total number of refugees including the owner's household could not have exceeded three hundred. From there, the tornado proceeded to the crowded Clothing Depot.

According to later estimates based on the condition of the few trees that remained standing in the garden, the height to which objects in them or elsewhere had been carried, the extent to which zinc sheets were bent and similar indications, the storm was revolving at about the speed mentioned by Dr. Imamura, of some 70 meters a second. Meanwhile, the speed at which it was progressing across the ground was only 10 or 15 meters a second, or between 20 and 30 miles an hour. At this leisurely pace, assuming that the pillar of the storm was, as Professor Imamura's calculations suggested, 300 yards thick at the base, and also allowing for some indirection in its course, the tornado must have been in and over the area for several minutes. In any case, it was there long enough to ignite everything that was inflammable; and either the flames or the carbon monoxide or a combination of both were sufficient to dispose of practically everyone present. Of the 40,000 refugees who had been in the Depot when the tornado swept over it, the survivors were a few hundred who had been buried under other bodies or who had been at an edge of the area which was outside the storm's rim.

The spot where Makiko had obediently taken up her stand three hours earlier, with her beach towel tied to a stick as an improvised flag, was not far from the southern, or downstream, entrance to the Depot. She and the four factory workers who had come with her stayed there, letting the crowds that continued to pour into the area shuffle past them toward the center of the Depot, which was filling up rapidly. Clearly the center of the space appeared the best place to be in case the fire were to press in from three sides, but Makiko was determined to wait near the entrance at least until the other members of the family arrived. Anyhow, the idea that fire might eventually become a serious threat seemed to her most improbable.

About half an hour after Makiko had reached the Depot, her brother and a small cousin turned up with four more of the factory workers. They had spotted the makeshift flag and recognized it, just as Makiko had expected, and they pushed through the crowd to join her. The whole group now stayed near the entrance, looking for Mr. Aoki who they thought might presently join them too. Meanwhile, they watched the crowds that kept on coming in and finding places for themselves and for their belongings, somehow or other. They came singly or in groups, many pulling carts that were piled high with bedding, clothes, pots and pans, china, small pieces of furniture, even bird cages. Most of the women had babies tied on their backs in the customary fashion, as did many of the older children. Patients from nearby hospitals were carried in on stretchers or were supported by nurses as they hobbled along, looking dazed and pitiful. Makiko noticed a man with a horse-drawn wagon, loaded down with household goods; a very old man with a silvery goatee; several schoolboys wearing their new black uniforms just issued for the fall term.

Nowhere in the area was there the slightest sign of panic or even of serious alarm. On the contrary, it was as though experience with the Flowers of Edo through many centuries had planted in Tokyo people a sort of intuitive knowledge of how to cope with such situations whenever they arose. Realizing that their houses would be burned down and also that, in consequence, they would have to spend surely one and perhaps several nights in the open, many brought not only all the valuables and furniture they could carry on carts, bicycles or shoulder poles, but also overnight conveniences, like food boxes and straw mats or cushions to put on the ground.

When they reached some tenable position within the Depot, people tried to make themselves as comfortable as possible. Everyone was extremely polite; there was a minimum of pushing and shoving toward preferred spots. The ground was still quivering much of the time, but most of those present were familiar enough with earthquakes to know that these were mere aftershocks, never as bad as the first one and never really destructive. No one seemed to be much frightened by the threat of the fire; the feeling was that, by following the sensible instructions of the authorities, they had escaped the danger if not the inconvenience and the hardship. Now there was nothing to do but watch the flames from a distance and wait it out until a day or so later when they could go home again and start rebuilding. Meanwhile strangers conversed with each other, exchanging stories about their experiences in the morning's quake. Someone said he was sorry that he had not brought along a chess set.

In the excitement of departure, Makiko had, of course, finally failed to get any lunch. She watched, not without envy, as some refugees nearby unwrapped and opened the box of rice balls and fruit which they had judiciously brought with them. Photographers, presumably from some newspaper or other, turned up and began taking pictures of the Depot. The scene looked like a vast encampment; it was full of life and movement, the sound of people talking and calling to each other, of children laughing, crying in hunger or shouting in some game.

As the afternoon wore on, the bitter taste of smoke in the air grew stronger and the sky grew darker. There were huge clouds in the sky; seen through the smoky haze, they looked like thunderheads and someone said that perhaps a shower would come to put the fire out. Makiko realized suddenly, with a kind of futile indignation, that not only her family's house but her own new special room would certainly burn down. From time to time there was a sound of distant explosions. Someone said it must be Koreans, taking advantage of the catastrophe to make trouble.

Makiko's recollections of what happened a few seconds later, quite suddenly and without warning, were surprisingly coherent:

Suddenly I felt a shock—as though the entire Depot were in a whirl. There was no room to sit. People were standing one behind another, packed like sardines. I really do not know how it happened but people started falling down in piles. There was pandemonium. Most probably, fire had started. I grabbed my brother and my cousin and we all crouched. It got dark. I heard people praying. We were amidst a shower of fire flakes. I thought that I was going to die.

Since we were late in arriving at the Depot, we were not far from the entrance. As I hid myself beside a heap of human bodies, I suddenly noticed a horse growing wild. It looked like some sort of an apparition. Suddenly, something started burning right by my side. That is when I was burnt, though I did not know it at the time. "Fire!" I cried, and dragged my brother and cousin out of the heap of human bodies. The next moment, both of them had disappeared. A terrific wind had started blowing; they must both have been blown away.

I could not help running. I hit myself against something and fainted. I came to myself and found that I was standing on a heap of human bodies. Again, I was blown away. I was running but suddenly I couldn't see anything. I thought that I must have become blind. I was being dragged along. I fell down. I fainted. Someone ran into me.

I remember being in this sort of situation about three times. I made up my mind not to get up the next time. I was choking and forever running. Then I felt a sudden urge to live. I raised my hair with the palm of my hand and realized that I was not blind. I ran toward the river. I saw a well but since I was running against my will I had to pass it by. I fell down and became sleepy but woke up, hurt by fire flakes. I started running again. I came to a puddle and buried my face in the muddy water. I was beside a pond, the pond of the Yasuda residence.

I raised my face and realized that the wind had stopped blowing. I was myself again. I had lost one shoe. I took off the other and threw it away. As it was safer in the water, I waded into the pond. . . .

CHAPTER VI

RYUGENHIGO

FLOWING OF EVIL WORDS

THAT WIND and whirlwind should have played an important part in the earthquake-fire was in keeping with Japanese tradition. Winds have more than once had a major role in Japan's history— most notably the famous *kamikaze,* or divine wind, which destroyed the invasion fleet of Kublai Khan when he set out from Korean ports to conquer Japan in 1281. For that matter, Korea, too, became involved with the Great Kanto Earthquake—in a way which a rapid glance at more recent history may help to clarify.

When, after the two and a half centuries of seclusion imposed by the Tokugawa shoguns, Japan was somewhat brusquely introduced into the comity of nations by the gunboat invitation of Admiral Perry in 1853, the Japanese showed characteristic deftness in adjusting to this unexpected turn of events. First, noting that Great Britain had readily defeated China in the so-called Opium War of 1839-42, they realized that the Orient was in many important ways behind the times and took effective steps —like the fact-finding commission of 1861—to remedy this condition. Second, having studied the habits of great powers, the

Japanese not unreasonably concluded, as early as 1876, that it might be suitable for them to begin to act like a great power also. Korea was near at hand, far more backward than Japan and not yet claimed by any Western interloper. Patterning their behavior upon Western models, the Japanese decided to transmit to Korea those same benefits of commercial enlightenment that the West has so recently conferred upon Japan. The procedure employed was naturally the one they had just learned from Perry—that of having a cordial invitation to sign a treaty of amity and commerce conveyed by warship.

Unfortunately for all concerned, Japan's invitation to Korea had quite different results from that of the United States to Japan. Instead of responding gratefully, its beneficiaries proved surly, intractable and at last openly hostile. Thus, after assuring themselves a free hand in the matter, by demolishing the Russian fleet at Tsushima Strait in 1905, Japan felt justified in making Korea a "protectorate" in 1907. Korea's most dedicated nationalist, a young man named Syngman Rhee, moved to Washington, D. C., where one of his first acts was to acquire a national seal which, as first president of his native land, he would need for the first time some thirty-nine years later.

For Japan, the job of governing Korea proved to be a headache from the start, and the headache grew more acute after the First World War. The difficulty was one in which political hostility was emphasized by temperamental incompatibility; the Koreans heated even the floors of their houses in wintertime, and they ate stews that were not only smelly but also most untidy in appearance. Friction came to a head in 1919 when, on September 2, the Governor and his Inspector General—a man named Rentaro Mizuno—became the targets of a bomb thrown by a "secessionist" in Seoul. The Governor escaped uninjured but two reporters were killed and Rentaro Mizuno quite severely wounded.

During the period that followed, further difficulties developed such as those attending a land-reform law introduced by the Inspector General. As a preface to this reform, all landowners were required to register their holdings by a certain date. When many small landowners failed to comply—the Japanese authorities had perhaps understandably overlooked the detail that most Korean squires, unlike those at home, were illiterate—they automatically lost their property and were reduced to tenant farming. Since rents were exorbitant and since Japanese contractors were offering good wages for unskilled workers in Tokyo and Yokohama, many of the dispossessed farmers accepted such employment. In both cities these disgruntled emigrés lived in slums where their social status was comparable to that of colored stevedores in Mississippi or the Puerto Rican set on New York's Park Avenue. As for Rentaro Mizuno, his wounds helped to accelerate his rise as a public servant. Recalled to the capital, he became Home Minister in the Cabinet just preceding the one that Admiral Count Yamamoto was trying to form on the morning of Nihyaku-toka.

The formation of that Cabinet, like everything else in the vicinity, was disrupted by the earthquake. The Admiral started down the stairs of the Naval Club, but before he could reach the ground floor, a wall collapsed and the falling plaster injured his left arm. As he came out into the garden, Kenzo Fukuma, the *Asahi* reporter, noticed that he was rubbing dirt off his sleeve and asked whether he had been badly hurt. The Admiral replied only, "Well, you certainly will have plenty to write about today."

A Cabinet was finally formed the next day, in which, as anticipated, Viscount Goto accepted the portfolio of Home Affairs. Its investiture and first meeting were held on the lawn of the so-called "Detached Palace" in the Akasaka district—a grandiose copy of Versailles whose incongruity had never been more conspicuous. Meanwhile, the outgoing Cabinet had been obliged to take the first steps in dealing with the emergency. One of these was to secure from the Chairman of the Privy Council permission to declare martial law. The Chairman was found by the Cabinet Secretary, after a ten-mile bicycle ride, sitting on a broken door in the garden of his suburban villa. It thus came about that the last official act of Home Minister Rentaro Mizuno, before handing over his duties to Count Goto, was that of issuing instructions to the Commander of the Tokyo garrison. In these instructions, the question of the behavior of the Korean immigrants in Tokyo was no doubt touched upon—all the more surely since the day after the disaster had, among its other distinctions, that of being the anniversary of the attempted assassination of Mizuno four years earlier.

The question of precisely what the outgoing Home Minister may have said to the Army Commander in making him responsible for law and order in the metropolitan district has never—in the understandable absence of normal documentation—been satisfactorily established. It assumes considerable significance nonetheless in view of certain other developments that were taking place at more or less the same time. These developments started with a sudden crop of astonishingly virulent and widespread rumors to the effect that the Korean immigrants were taking advantage of the catastrophe in every possible way, from ordinary looting to marshaling an army that was said to be marching on the capital.

The rumors about the Koreans produced immediate and violent reactions. In Tokyo and Yokohama and the suburbs between and around them—especially those which had been least severely damaged by the quake and the fires—gangs of vigilantes were formed, apparently with the approval of the military authorities and certainly with the enthusiastic cooperation of the *Seinendan,* or Youth Corps. These vigilantes armed themselves with old samurai swords, bamboo spears, clubs, pikestaffs and kitchen knives. Posting themselves at important intersections, they established roadblocks to search for Koreans. On finding them, they held drumhead trials and in many cases disposed of them on the spot.

Beginning with the night of September 1 and for several days thereafter, thousands of homeless citizens of Tokyo and Yokohama, especially the former, were roaming the smoldering ruins in the effort to find their families. Other thousands were trying to leave the urban area on foot and walk to villages where they had relatives who might be able to provide food and shelter. Among the homeless were, of course, almost all the Korean immigrants, who, since they had no sources of succor outside the cities and in many cases did not even know how to ask for help in Japanese, may well have been guilty of looting burned-out shops for edible remnants of food. Among them too were hundreds of prisoners who had been released from jail—either intentionally, because of the threat of fire, or involuntarily, as in the case of many in Yokohama where prison walls had crashed with the earthquake. Under these conditions, the vigilantes found ample opportunity to show their mettle and made the most of it. One method of interrogation frequently applied to vagrants suspected of being Koreans was to require them to recite the common Japanese syllabary, "Ba, bi, bu, be, bo." Koreans could be counted on to give the b's the sound of p's; and many needed only to qualify as such before being stabbed, sliced, or beaten to death.

Since Koreans in Japan—unlike victims of race prejudice in most other countries—are likely to be more or less indistinguishable in appearance from their persecutors, confusion characterized these atrocities. Many of the victims were undoubtedly not Koreans at all but Japanese in such a state of shock or terror that their replies to interrogation were sufficiently tongue-tied to suit the purposes of the vigilantes—whose main objective was often simply to find victims. Others qualified on even more dubious grounds. The most distressing case of all was perhaps that of two teen-age children skewered on homemade bamboo spears, who were later identified as members of the first graduating class of Japan's aural school for the deaf. Halting enunciation of their native tongue, combined with inability to comprehend the questions shouted at them by the vigilantes, understandably failed to satisfy the latter, who had found these victims searching for their parents in the Tokyo ruins.

A more typical incident was later recalled by a small boy who heard whimpering noises beneath the floor of a Buddhist temple where his family had taken refuge on the outskirts of town. Thinking to find a dog, he raised a loose plank.

I found myself looking at a man who said in a strange rasping voice, "Have pity on me. My leg is broken. If they find me, they will kill me." A few minutes later, my father came in and said, "There is panic about the Koreans. Do you remember when the fire started? They say it was dynamite thrown by the Koreans." My pity for the man under the floor diminished. I was about to reveal his whereabouts when I heard people shouting outside, "He ran into the graveyard. Catch him! Kill him!" Footsteps of the vigilantes came into the temple. "Here he is!" I heard a terrible cry. . . .

Though most of the atrocities were committed by teen-age members of the vigilante gangs, there were some noteworthy exceptions. One of these took place in a rice field on the outskirts of Tokyo, where a factory worker reported having seen soldiers tie the hands of seven Koreans behind their backs and then beat their prisoners to death with rifle butts.

Participation by the Army in at least some of the atrocities, combined with the fact that Rentaro Mizuno had been the Home Minister responsible for instituting martial law, had an important bearing on one of the lasting consequences of the disaster. This was the belief—which, baseless or otherwise, obtained wide currency— that the Army had been told to expect trouble from the Koreans, to warn the populace, and to encourage the vigilante groups. In denying these allegations, the military authorities later stated that, on the contrary, their orders had been to counteract the rumors by explaining that in most cases they were unfounded, to trace down their origin whenever possible, and to arrest parties guilty of spreading them, when they could be ascertained.

The best evidence that the Army did not start the rumors is simply that they had begun to circulate almost twenty-four hours before martial law was established. Nonetheless, it is also true that the Yamamoto government, pleading higher priority for relief and reconstruction, failed to conduct a full-scale investigation of the atrocities and to provide appropriate punishment for those responsible. The result is that no one yet knows even approximately how many helpless Koreans were massacred in the first day or two after the earthquake. Korean sources in Japan claim that the number was upward of 6,000; government sources indicate that there might have been as many as 500 victims of every description done to death in the period of mass hysteria. The true figure at a rough guess might lie between 500 and 1,000 Koreans, but the actual number is perhaps less important than the final consequence of the whole affair. This was a widespread conviction among Koreans that the Japanese government had condoned, if it had not actually caused, the atrocities. This conviction has endured to help poison relations between the two countries ever since.

What did cause the rumors about the Koreans and how did they really start? For some days before the earthquake, the newspapers had carried more stories than usual about unrest in Korea and its potential repercussions among the Korean immigrants in Japan. Many fires were in fact touched off by accidental explosions, in drugstores and school laboratories, of chemicals released by breakage during the quake. These circumstances combined to make extensive sabotage seem plausible. Added to this was the special readiness of human beings, in circumstances which combined disaster with mass assembly, to absorb and to pass along misinformation of every kind. Police investigations showed that immediately after the earthquake, many reports of many different sorts were circulated so widely that some of them eventually found their way around the world. In downtown Tokyo, there were word-of-mouth warnings that a giant tidal wave was about to engulf the city; that

Mount Fuji was in such violent eruption that the capital would soon be entombed like Pompeii in a flood of lava; that another, and more violent, earthquake could be expected at any moment.

While all these reports were proved false within a few hours, they served nonetheless to increase general apprehension and susceptibility to dismal forebodings. In the absence of newspapers— the plants of all but one had been burned out, and even that one, the *Nichi Nichi,* lacked any means of distribution—no reliable source of information existed, just when public need for it was most intense. Irresponsible individuals found it easy to bolster their own waning confidence by posing as oracles: their listeners were in a mood to credit any fearsome predictions, and the more horrifying they were the more appropriate and plausible they became.

Finally, according to later diagnosis by psychiatrists, complicated subconscious motivations were at work. Along with terror and confusion, the quake and the fire created feelings, often repressed, of bitter anger against the injustice of circumstance or fate. In order to be released, this repressed anger needed a target and the Koreans were the handiest one available.

The stories multiplied and grew in telling. People whispered that the Koreans had used the real earthquake fires as a cover for mass incendiarism; that was why the conflagration had spread so fast. Years before, when Tokyo's water system had been installed, the municipal authorities had requested residents to fill in all private wells; now the few wells that remained were desperately needed. It was said that the Koreans were poisoning these, or throwing children into them. The great army that the Koreans were mobilizing in the neighborhood of the Tamagawa River, halfway between Tokyo and Yokohama, would soon be marching on both towns. . . .

It was the patent absurdity of this last canard which, more than anything else, helped to put a stop to the whole uproar. The notion that a few thousand Koreans in a strange land could possibly constitute a serious military menace clearly belonged in a class with the earlier false alarms about tidal waves, eruptions and climactic quakes. It died down rapidly and with it most of the others on the same subject. By the third day after the quake, the Korean scare was over and the police had in fact established a barracks outside the city where some ten thousand of the immigrants received shelter, sustenance and protection.

FOR BASELESS SLANDER and malicious rumor the familiar Japanese term is *ryugenhigo,* or flowing of evil words. As the ryugenhigo began to subside, the flow was replaced by more reliable accounts of some of the things that had really happened during the first day or two of the disaster. Confronted with any sort of extraordinary conditions, for which their almost ritualistic social discipline makes no provision, the Japanese are always likely to manifest extreme reactions. Fortunately, these extremes usually extend in both directions. The appalling hysteria about the Koreans was of brief duration, confined to a few areas, and manifested mainly by a small minority composed of Seinendan members whose ferocity was usually in inverse ratio to the degree to which they themselves had suffered in the quake. No less noteworthy in their way were the reactions of the vast majority of the population, which included numerous examples of very different behavior by those who had been most deeply involved in the catastrophe.

Europeans who lived through the quake paid unanimous tribute to the exemplary courage and calm with which the Japanese in general confronted the catastrophe. Panic was rare. Looting was at a minimum. The huge crowds that survived the terrible first night of fire in the public parks of Tokyo and Yokohama were for the most part remarkably well disciplined. Instances of unusual courage or common sense under extreme stress were numerous.

Among the institutions that especially distinguished themselves were Tokyo's hospitals, whose nurses and doctors saved thousands of patients under almost impossible conditions. One example was that of Tokyo's Municipal Charity Hospital, located on the Sumida River and bounded on three sides by a bend in the stream and on the fourth by the Naval College. Most of the staff doctors and nurses, thinking the hospital safe from fire and tidal waves, departed at five o'clock. A resident doctor, a clerk, a pharmacist and fifty-four nurses were left to care for some two hundred patients. At eight o'clock in the evening, helped by the shifting of the wind, the fire jumped the river above the hospital; when the flames reached the Naval College, it was only a matter of time until the hospital caught too. What made its position especially perilous was the presence of six powder magazines on the property of the college. These were sure to explode as soon as the fire reached them.

Seven of the nurses helped thirty-two of the least seriously ill patients into the river and, using the long sashes of their kimonos to tie themselves to an anchored barge, managed to support their charges in the water through the early hours of the night. Meanwhile the clerk saw a small empty barge floating down the river. He swam out to it, seized the charred towline in his teeth and swam back with it to the hospital landing. On this barge, aided by the resident doctor and the pharmacist, he made three trips across the river, evacuating all the patients without casualty—the last ones a few minutes before the powder magazines began to explode, blowing the hospital to bits.

On Tokyo's great central shopping street, the Ginza, the central point is the Nihon Bashi, or Japan Bridge, from which the distance to the capital of other points is officially reckoned. Near this bridge stood the solid stone building of the Sumitomo Bank, which, like almost all other stone buildings in the capital, stood through the earthquake with relatively little damage. Since the quake occurred just before Saturday closing time, the staff might well have departed immediately afterward. Instead, most of its members stayed on until three o'clock, using files, hammers and crowbars to close the heavy steel shutters over window frames that had been bent just enough to impair the fit. Shoichi Hiraga, whose regular job was to supervise the closing of the vaults, then dismissed the entire staff except for nine guards with whom he stayed on in the sealed building.

Late in the afternoon, as the fire closed in on the Ginza, refugees swarmed up to the front door. Hiraga admitted several dozen of them, but presently a police car drove past in which an officer with a megaphone was shouting that everyone in the area must flee at once to the Imperial Palace Plaza. The refugees departed and with them—at Hiraga's order—five of the guards. Hiraga and the other four stayed on.

As the fire surrounded the pitch-dark building, the air inside became so hot that the men could barely breathe. Stripped to their shorts, they sat together in the main conference room containing the safe, as smoke seeped through cracks in the bent shutters. The sound of the flames outside and of nearby buildings crashing to the ground was followed by even more terrifying noises: roofing tiles, metal sheets and other heavy objects were being hurled against the walls by a fiery whirlwind.

At two o'clock in the morning, while this was going on, the building rocked and shook in the night's heaviest aftershock. According to an hourly record that Hiraga was able to write by the light of the fire coming through the cracks, this was the worst moment of the night. By 5 A.M., all the other buildings in the neighborhood had burned to the ground and the Ginza itself, paved with wooden blocks, was a bed of ashes. Now the air in the bank became perceptibly cooler and at seven, the occupants crept to the front door and cautiously opened it a few inches. On the doorstep were the five guards who had gone to the Palace Plaza and who had now returned to try to rescue their colleagues. The Sumitomo Bank was the first in Tokyo to reopen for business, on September 8.

In Tokyo Central Station, a noteworthy job of preservation and rescue work was accomplished by Yoshinosuke Okamoto, in charge of the Railway Engine House. Anticipating the need for special trains to evacuate refugees after the fire, he began by trying to keep up boiler-pressure in his engines until he learned that even to the north of the city, damage to the tracks had made them impassable. This raised the question of storing all the trains then in the station so that they would be ready for use later, when the tracks had been repaired. Locating spur lines and sidings that were accessible and relatively safe, he got most of the trains onto them. In many cases, this meant that the engineers had to run their engines into flaming areas and then hold them there while yardmen, themselves working in the scorching heat, pulled the switches that would enable the trains to back away.

By 5 A.M., a hundred trains had been pulled into safety. Now came the problem of how to handle more than 3,000 refugees who had crowded into the station from nearby burned-out areas. Okamoto made room for them not only in the station but in storage sheds and in the parked trains. Berths were removed for use as cots for the ill and injured. Several babies were born in the trains with conductors acting as midwives. Rice from the commissary was used to make gruel—a cup for each refugee. Yard workers did their best to clean up the lavatories—where water pressure had stopped with the quake—using water from a nearby drainage canal. On the fourth day after the earthquake, a communal hot bath was set up in which fifteen people at a time were allowed to bathe. A few days later, the tracks to the north of the city had been restored sufficiently for the first refugees to start leaving on the trains saved from destruction at the station yards.

While all the animals in the Ueno Park Zoo, Tokyo's largest,

survived the fire safely, those in the smaller Hanayashiki Zoo, attached to the Asakusa amusement park, were less fortunate. What
happened to them was reported by their head keeper, Torizo Fukui,
when he appeared at the nearby Asakusa Temple, leading a small
eleven-year-old elephant who later became the pet of several thousand refugees in the temple grounds:

Hanayashiki Zoo was surrounded by fire. Using a hose, I was trying
my best to save as many animals as possible. I didn't even think of my
own safety. Suddenly it dawned on me what would happen if the wild
animals got into a panic in this chaos. Although I've taken care of and
loved each one of them, I got a pistol and began shooting them.

When I got to the elephant's cage, I could not bring myself to kill the
sixty-two-year-old one; he was so gentle and meek. I continued pouring
water on him with the hose, but it was no use. The straw roofing of the
cage caught fire and he died of suffocation. Then I went over to the
carpenter's shed where the little eleven-year-old one was taking shelter.
There was no time to pour water on him, so I broke the chain and set
him free. He was so panic-stricken that he couldn't even move. I dragged
him out of the fire and brought him here. Please be kind to him.

One of the most renowned heroes of the disaster was John Laffin,
the thirty-two-year-old son of a former American clipper-ship officer
and his Japanese wife, who, with his father, was credited with effective rescue work in the harbor at Yokohama. When the quake
started, young Laffin, an enthusiastic yachtsman, had just finished a
repair job on his 38-foot cruiser and was testing the motor a few
yards offshore to see if it worked more smoothly. When the whole
boat began to shake and buck, he thought his tinkering had had a
catastrophic effect and hurriedly switched off the ignition. Only
then did he hear the roar of falling buildings and realize that the
trouble was not confined to his cockpit.

Laffin put in to shore, brought supplies of food and fresh water
from his house and came back to his boat. That afternoon, and
throughout the next thirty-six hours, he and his father, who had a

similar cruiser and used it for the same purpose, ferried hundreds of injured refugees from the shore to the larger ships in the harbor. It was Laffin who carried the *André LeBon*'s hawser out to the harbor buoy, enabling the liner to winch herself away from the pier before the flames reached her.

Even the Koreans were, in some cases, the beneficiaries of Japanese loyalty and courage. A case in point was Han Hyon San, who, as an anarchist and subsequently vice-president of the Koreans Association in Japan, was later instrumental in publishing the gravest charges against the government. He owed his life to the protection of his Japanese teacher, who sheltered him in his house for a month after the disaster.

ACCORDING TO A THEORY advanced by William James—confirmed by the San Francisco earthquake and fire of 1906, of which he was a witness—leadership in great emergencies is most likely to come from unexpected sources. Authorities, officials, major executives in big organizations, and others who are thoroughly accustomed to directing the course of events may grow so disconcerted when events resist their directives that they become less useful just when they should become more so. Conversely, humble citizens, whose abilities, concealed by the ordinary run of affairs, have remained untested, may find in crisis the long-awaited opportunity to show their true capacities.

In the Great Kanto Earthquake, the behavior of hundreds of obscure individuals tended to confirm this theory. On the other hand, the behavior of many seasoned administrators partially belied it. One of the latter was Tetsuzo Inumaru, the manager of the Imperial Hotel, who, in accord with the theory, should have gone to pieces soon after the first shock. On the contrary, what happened was that his lifetime habit of handling the small crises of which a hotelman's life is largely composed enabled him to confront this tremendous one with his customary aplomb.

Having extinguished the fire in the kitchen, Inumaru instructed his cooks to forget about the banquet and use charcoal fires to prepare instead a large quantity of *satsumajiru,* a kind of soupy, sweet-potato stew which is a standard Japanese form of emergency ration. He then set off for the banquet hall where he arrived just as the electric fans began raining down from the balcony in a major aftershock that occurred at 12:15.

The principal danger to the hotel, Inumaru saw at once, would be that of fire; two buildings across the street were already in flames although fortunately the wind was carrying the flames away from the hotel. Inumaru ordered the floor staff to close all the windows. He then organized bucket brigades to draw water from the lily pond—installed by Wright in the entrance courtyard over the protests of the directors—and use it to wet down the Imperial's roof. Having done so, the bucket brigade also helped to extinguish one of the two fires across the street. That evening, fire approached the Imperial from another direction, but just as it seemed inevitable that the hotel would catch, the wind changed and carried the flames off to the south. Inumaru's memoirs indicate that, having ensured the safety of his guests, he then turned his attention to their comfort.

The first night there had been the danger from the fire. The second night there was the scare about the raiders. There were thousands of refugees in Hibiya Park, just across the street. What would they do if they could not get food? Or if it should rain? There had been no rain for several days. The weather was still warm enough to sleep out of doors.

Well, the day after the earthquake, there was some fighting and raiding in the city, and wild rumors began to go around—of large bands of raiders on the march. A Japanese official whispered to me that they

would aim at our hotel—now the commercial and political center—
and at Tokyo Station, to cut off all communications. Some reliable reports of trouble came to me. I have a friend who is a sort of Robin Hood,
and he brought his men to help me protect the hotel. With several Am-
bassadors here and many other foreigners, we had to take special pre-
cautions. Our whole staff armed themselves with whatever they could
find and kept guard all that night.

In the evening I sent a letter to the Captain of the Guard asking for
soldiers to protect the hotel. His answer was that soldiers are not sent by
request of private persons but by order—that they would be sent if the
military authorities found it necessary. So I went and said, "Well, how
do they find out when it is necessary? If they find out the necessity, it is
too late. In home affairs we can suppress things, but if an affair is international it goes by wireless to foreign countries. For this international
affair why can't you send soldiers? It is not my business to keep guard."
I could not get soldiers, so I went to the Foreign Office the next morning,
and they sent thirty right away and more later. That night I slept.

Another executive type who rose to the occasion in the same
admirable style was the wily Greek, Antonios Pappadopoulos. The
first shock of the quake had knocked him down as he was on his
way to the tramline. He struggled to his feet and ran back across the
shaking earth to his house, in the ruins of which he found his wife
and two small children. Pappadopoulos was able to extricate them
along with a few personal possessions which included a cello, a case
of rum, and the defective movie camera. He then assembled
his family and the wives of four neighbors, who seemed to be at the
point of hysteria, near a small tree in a nearby field, tethered them
all to the tree, and forced each of the women to gulp a swallow or
two of straight rum to keep their courage up. Presently, several
others joined their group.

Not far from the Pappadopoulos house, which was on a small
separate eminence near the Bluff, was the Negishi Prison, which
had been destroyed by the quake and from which the prisoners had
been released on parole, to enable them to escape the fire. It was
said that there was sure to be looting; that the prisoners would look

for places where fresh earth showed that people had buried valuables; that the Koreans would be on the rampage. Pappadopoulos went back to his house to get his revolver and some ammunition. This time, pushing his arm through a smashed window, he secured the ammunition but just as he put his hand on the weapon, an aftershock shifted the ruins just enough to pin his arm in place. Pappadopoulos tried to call for help but found he could do so only in German, which was the last of the five languages he had picked up in the course of his varied career. No help came, but eventually, thanks to another aftershock, he freed his hand, with the weapon in it.

Before the quake, the Pappadopoulos hen house had contained fifty fat pullets and one scrawny old rooster named Beelzebub. The hen house had collapsed in the quake and all the pullets had escaped, cackling madly and flapping their wings in furious efforts to fly. Beelzebub, however—though his usefulness was obviously at an end—was still much in evidence; too much in evidence, Pappadopoulos, who had always detested the old fowl, suddenly decided. Usually an expert revolver shot, he now fired six times before he managed to put a bullet through the rooster's neck. Then he took the carcass and, still speaking in ceremonious German, presented it to the group of ladies, who cooked it for lunch. That evening the husbands of two of them joined the group; by then it was apparent that the other two women had become widows.

During the afternoon, two local policemen—out of uniform because, they explained, escaped prisoners and looters were killing uniformed policemen on sight—joined the encampment. Shelter was improvised out of dislodged doors and bits of broken roofing; food supplies and bedding were extricated from wrecked houses and given to the women. Toward evening, more survivors appeared, and Pappadopoulos—who had gradually recovered his linguistic versatility—found himself in command of a sort of improvised international brigade. At dusk, a band of some three dozen marauders

approached the encampment, demanding food or money. Pappadopoulos dispersed them by shooting over their heads.

On Sunday, word got out that a detachment of marines from the
base at Yokosuka had been landed and that they had thrown a
cordon around Yokohama in a semicircle with a six-mile radius.
They were going to round up the escaped prisoners and other law-
less elements. During the afternoon, Pappadopoulos and his group
heard rifle shots, first at a distance, then closer. In the evening, the
sounds were near at hand and with them were mingled screams of
terror and pain. It appeared from these that escapees were being
shot, clubbed or speared to death. Toward midnight, a naked Japanese, wild-eyed, bloody and dripping with sweat, came running
out of the darkness to beg protection. The policemen in the group,
convinced that the man was an escaped prisoner, were all for
killing him on the spot. Pappadopoulos restrained them and gave
the fugitive a chance to run back into the darkness. This act of
mercy diminished his authority over the group. By dawn on Monday morning, its members separated and Pappadopoulos made his
way through the ruined city to the waterfront.

In both Tokyo and Yokohama, especially the former, Sunday
was given over by a large part of the population to the search for
missing relatives. At midday on Saturday, when the earthquake
had occurred, most families were naturally scattered and since then
fires, death, and the breakdown of all transport and communication
had kept them so. Now the searchers wandered about the smoking
ruins, calling each other's names or carrying on long sticks signs
bearing the names of those who were missing. Public monuments
were designated as bulletin boards for family notices; thousands of
these, crudely lettered on bits of cardboard or torn paper, were fixed
to the pedestals of statues in the parks or to the façades of public
buildings. Most helpless of all the searchers were the lost children,
of whom several thousand, cared for at first by other refugees, were
later turned over to the authorities. Most of these were even-

tually restored to their parents or to other relatives; a few hundred, whose parents were never found, were placed in special homes for earthquake foundlings.

Makiko Aoki was among the lucky ones. During the night, she had found a group of people hiding under a wet quilt as protection against heat and the falling fire flakes. In daylight, she found that one of the people under this quilt, by an amazing chance, was a girl in her class at school. They had been talking to each other early on Saturday morning, when both had gone to the school to draw their fall-term textbooks. Makiko and her schoolmate decided to go together to look for the bodies of their families. Two men from the group who had a similar errand offered to join them.

The four started their search at the Depot where what seemed to be numberless bodies were heaped up, some of them still squirming slightly or making unintelligible noises. Most of the bodies were burned black but some were burned slightly and some, apparently, not burned at all. The searchers came to a canal where they found a small boat. The men suggested that they sit down in it to rest. While they were sitting there in the boat, other people who were also looking for lost relatives walked past on the bank. Among these passers-by, Makiko presently saw a woman whom she knew—an elderly neighbor who was a friend of her grandmother. She called to the woman, who told her that she had seen her grandmother, alive and uninjured, a few minutes before. Makiko went where the neighbor directed her and found her grandmother; together they continued the search for the rest of the family. The next day they were encountered by Mr. Aoki, who had Makiko's little brother with him. Mr. Aoki had been one of the survivors on the Shin-Ohashi Bridge, guarded by Policeman Gensaku Hatori.

Dr. Ikeguchi had spent the night on a boat in the river, lying in the bilge water to dull the pain of his burns. His hands, from which most of the flesh had been scorched away, were entirely useless, but someone else in the boat mercifully fed him a slice of watermelon. In the morning, he got back on shore and went to the Yasuda garden to see if the things he remembered about the night before were really true.

They were all true. A man came by while the doctor was looking at the burned bodies of his wife and children. The doctor asked this man to take a name-card and the pencil he used for writing prescriptions out of the pocket of his black alpaca coat. The man got them out of the pocket and then, at the doctor's request, wrote a message on the card. The message was that no one was to touch the bodies and that the doctor himself would return to attend to them. The doctor then requested the man to attach the card to a stick and to put the stick across the four bodies. The man did this. Dr. Ikeguchi thanked him and walked back toward the river.

CHAPTER VII

NANA-KOROBI ...

SEVEN TIMES FALL DOWN

MONG THOSE not actually in the area of the Great Kanto Earthquake, one of the first people to be aware of it was one of those farthest away. This was the Reverend Father Francis A. Tondorf, director of the Seismological Station at Georgetown University in Washington, D. C. He learned about it—or at least learned that there had been a major seismic disturbance of some sort on the opposite side of the world, probably in Japan—at 10:12 on the evening of August 31, by Eastern standard time, or about fourteen minutes after the earthquake occurred. Other seismographs had recorded the disturbance shortly before that—at Vienna eleven minutes after the quake; at Hong Kong, five and a half. However, while these records indicated about how far away the quake was, and that it was of the first magnitude, none of them indicated much more than that. For even the sketchiest account of the greatest catastrophe in history, the outside world had to wait over eleven hours, almost a full half-day.

In the circumstances, this delay in the transmission of the news of the quake was perhaps less remarkable than that the news got out at all—in bits and pieces which were relayed to the rest of the world by makeshift means over the next several days. The Great Kanto Earthquake Disaster was spread over such a wide area, it extended over such a wide range of developments, and it affected so many people and things, that, even if all communications had been in perfect working order, getting the story would have been a journalistic feat of heroic proportions. With all communications totally disrupted, it is scarcely surprising that nothing approaching the whole story, even in the most conventional sense of this term, reached the rest of the world within the first hours or days after the event—or, for that matter, ever.

The first effective attempt to communicate news of the disaster was that made by Police Chief Jiro Morioka of Yokohama, after spending an extraordinarily harrowing afternoon. Soon after the quake, refugees had begun crowding into the Prefectural Government Building where he had his office. When the building caught fire, Morioka herded the crowd through encircling flames to the waterfront where he got into the water just in time to encounter the first patches of blazing oil drifting down from the exploded Rising Sun tanks. He and the others plunged in nonetheless, to try to swim past the oil patches toward one of the larger ships. At 6:30, after three hours in the water, a launch, possibly one of the Laffins', picked up Morioka and transferred him to the Japanese freighter *Korea Maru* which had backed off from her pier and followed the *Philoctetes* through the breakwater to an anchorage two miles off shore. Shortly after being taken on board, he secured permission from the captain to use the ship's wireless to send out an appeal for help. In his message, the police chief made one serious error. He addressed it, optimistically, to the home office in Tokyo.

Fortunately, the same alertness that had caused Morioka to think of using the ship's wireless in the first place continued to operate. Concluding that the reason for Tokyo's failure to respond must be severe earthquake damage in that city also, he dispatched another message, to the Governor of Osaka, at about 9 P.M. It was this message that finally reached not only Osaka but also various other shore stations and ships at sea, thus setting in motion the first relief operations. The message has been reproduced in various translations, of which the most satisfactory reads as follows:

TODAY AT NOON A GREAT EARTHQUAKE OCCURRED AND WAS IMMEDIATELY FOLLOWED BY A CONFLAGRATION WHICH HAS CHANGED THE WHOLE CITY INTO A SEA OF FIRE, CAUSING COUNTLESS CASUALTIES. ALL FACILITIES OF TRAFFIC HAVE BEEN DESTROYED AND COMMUNICATIONS CUT OFF. WE HAVE NEITHER WATER NOR FOOD. FOR GOD'S SAKE SEND RELIEF AT ONCE.

Among the shore wireless stations that caught Morioka's message to Osaka was Iwaki, a small town some 150 miles northeast of Tokyo. The operator there, a man named Kaichiro Yonemura, had already become aware of the earthquake through fragmentary messages from other shore stations and from other ships at Yokohama. He was also aware that his was the only station in Japan capable of communicating with foreign countries. The tone of Morioka's message impressed Yonemura with the gravity of the situation at Yokohama. Knowing that many Europeans lived there, and realizing that he was now Japan's only communications link with the rest of the world, he decided that it was his duty to give out the news. This he did by composing in English a twenty-word message addressed to the Radio Corporation of America station at Los Angeles, which he sent at 11 P.M. This message, based on Morioka's and containing no mention of Tokyo, read as follows:

CONFLAGRATION SUBSEQUENT TO SEVERE EARTHQUAKE AT YOKOHAMA AT NOON TODAY. WHOLE CITY PRACTICALLY ABLAZE WITH NUMEROUS CASUALTIES. ALL TRAFFIC STOPPED.

Yonemura's message—in which "traffic" referred to cable, or telegraphic, traffic—was picked up by the RCA office in San

Francisco at 6:20 A.M. on Saturday, September 1, San Francisco time. RCA telephoned the news to the San Francisco office of the Associated Press, which, two minutes later, sent out a bulletin to all its subscribers. This bulletin, which began to appear in United States afternoon papers about twelve hours after the earthquake, was the first published news of the disaster.

For several days thereafter, newspapers all over the world were placed in the agonizing dilemma of being confronted by one of the biggest news stories of the century with no way of telling it. Aware that the score or so of correspondents in Tokyo had no means of getting messages out, the papers made every possible effort to communicate with the correspondents. In the attempt to reach its Tokyo bureau chief, George Denny, the AP radioed Yonemura to dispatch a courier; the courier reached Denny and came back three days later with the first eyewitness account of the disaster by a United States correspondent. Realizing that Yonemura was the key man in the situation, other papers had by this time cabled him for direct coverage, and Yonemura's stories, largely translated from Japanese provincial papers in nearby cities, were one of the world's main sources of information for the first week after the quake. Not surprisingly, some of the wilder rumors current in Tokyo found their way into his dispatches.

Among the less bizarre reports printed all over the world was that the quake had been accompanied, and perhaps caused, by a violent eruption of Mount Fuji. This persisted in one form or another until several days after the event when a group of three young ladies, one of whom was Miss Mary Alexander, the daughter of a Honolulu professor, turned up on one of the refugee ships in Kobe to contradict it. They had been in the midst of a tourist excursion on Fuji—about halfway up—when the quake struck. After many narrow escapes from big rocks and boulders which, dislodged by the shock, came rolling down the flank of the mountain at deadly speed, they and their guides had all reached the bottom safely.

More plausible than the eruption story but equally false was the report that the large island of Oshima at the entrance to Sagami Bay had vanished completely under the sea. In fact, although Oshima was probably closer to the epicenter of the quake than any point on the mainland, it suffered scarcely any damage at all—owing, apparently, to a geological character comprising peculiarly rigid and quake-resistant rock formations. The weirdest report of all was perhaps one that was conveyed in a small village on the Dutch-German border, to a Japanese schoolboy named Nagamasa Kawakita when he went to the telegraph office to send a message of inquiry to his family in Tokyo. The clerk refused to transmit it, saying, "It is impossible, your country is no more. But never mind, poor fellow. We Germans will take care of you here."

In regard to knowledge of what was happening in their capital and its environs, the Japanese themselves were not much better off than the rest of the world. The point farthest from its origin where the quake had lethal consequences was the mountain resort village of Karuizawa, 100 miles or so north of Tokyo. Here the shock was still strong enough to do minor damage to a few houses—in one of which a villager was killed by a falling beam. Among those summering at Karuizawa—a favorite resort of Europeans stationed in the capital, then as now—was B. W. Fleisher, proprietor of the renowned English-language *Japan Advertiser*. He was sufficiently impressed by the Karuizawa earthquake to address a telegram to his editor in Tokyo, telling him to stop the presses for a story about it.

Other residents of Karuizawa failed to connect the morning's shock with a strange phenomenon that came to their attention that evening. This was a strange and beautiful red glow along the southern horizon that many members of the summer colony spent hours watching from a rise in the ground near the village. One of the spectators was the distinguished American professor, Dr. Karl August Reischauer, for many years a member of the faculty at Meiji University in Tokyo, who concluded that the glow must have been caused by a new volcano in eruption.

Not until three days later, when refugees from the capital began to arrive on trains which they had caught by walking to a station several miles north of Tokyo, did Karuizawa learn what had really happened. First of these arrivals was an American businessman named Harold C. Huggins who had experienced not only the Tokyo quake but the San Francisco one seventeen years before. That evening he gave a talk in the Karuizawa town hall and, in comparing the two, said that the shocks were of about equal intensity. It was not until months afterward that Mrs. Reischauer learned something about the quake which was of especial significance to her. She was the founder and headmistress of the aural school for the deaf, whose two first graduates had been mistaken for Koreans.

Within the capital itself foreign correspondents adopted various expedients in the effort to cope with the biggest and most difficult story that they had ever had to cover. George Denny, before the messenger sent by Yonemura arrived from Iwaki, sent his copy to Nagoya where it was held up pending dispatch of government messages, which had priority. Other correspondents, aware that the Pacific cable connection to San Francisco via Honolulu was broken, made their way by foot to a railhead whence they could entrain for Nagasaki; there the Great Northern Cable Company might be able to move their stories via Vladivostok, Siberia, and Moscow. When they reached Nagasaki, the meticulous manager of the cable office refused their messages because they lacked the proper credentials for sending material collect from that office.

More resourceful than most were Denny's wire service rivals, the United Press and International News Service. Duke Parry, Tokyo correspondent for the latter, walked to Fujisusono, a village not far from Mount Fuji, whence the railroad tracks to Osaka were still clear. Trains were infrequent and packed with refugees, but he climbed onto the cowcatcher on the engine of the first one that left and got his story on the wire three days after the quake. The UP got prompter coverage than either of its rivals by enlisting the services of Moto Takata, a former New York correspondent for the Osaka *Mainichi*, who had been recalled to a post in his home office. The Osaka *Mainichi* was covering the story by sending its reporters to Tokyo in an airplane which then returned bringing staff members of its subsidiary, the Tokyo *Nichi Nichi*. Takata's first story—a rewrite in English of the eyewitness accounts thus obtained from the capital—was a thousand words which he sent at the full urgent rate of $3.50 each—the most expensive single message that the agency had ever received.

Japanese reporters in Tokyo also had their troubles. All but one of the major newspapers in Tokyo were burned out by mid-afternoon. That one, the *Nichi Nichi,* which burned later, printed only five hundred copies of a one-sheet handbill on the somewhat questionable premise that, under the circumstances, no one would want to read a paper anyway. The major papers transferred their important files, and as much office paraphernalia as could be carried away, to the Imperial Palace Plaza where they put up tents or sheds as temporary headquarters. For the *Asahi,* the problem was how to transmit the story to its Osaka office for publication in the Osaka edition. Kenzo Fukuma, the political reporter who had been covering the Cabinet-formation meeting at the Navy Club, was still eager to get in on something big. He volunteered to join one of the three teams, of three reporters each, who, late in the afternoon, set out for Osaka on foot, each by a different route. His team started last, at about six o' clock.

The three reporters walked out of Tokyo along the road to Yokohama and skirted the burning ruins of that city. When they reached Kamakura and saw what had happened there, one of the three, whose family lived nearby, decided that his prior obligation was to find out what had become of them. The other two continued walking through the night. The next morning, when they saw a plane overhead, Fukuma's companion deduced that it must be the *Asahi's* on its way to Osaka and that its arrival would make theirs superfluous. Fukuma was made of sterner stuff. He plowed on alone, following the railroad tracks and stopping only for three hours once for a nap in a freight car. Crossing the mountains near Hakone, he found most of the tunnels blocked by landslides. When thus impeded, he climbed over the mountain, picking up the tracks on the other side. At the entrance to many of the tunnels that were not blocked, he found vigilantes who warned him that the Koreans who were hiding inside would be sure to kill him. Fukuma, tired of climbing, went through anyway. There were no Koreans.

Somewhere along the way, Fukuma must have passed his colleague, Tatsuo Shiraishi, the *Asahi* driver who had been on the train derailed at Nebukawa by the landslide and who was walking the same track in the other direction. Had they met—they knew each other by sight—Shiraishi might have contributed a valuable addition to Fukuma's story, but they failed to do so.

On the evening of September 3, Fukuma reached the Fijisusono station, at the foot of Mount Fuji, from which the trains were still running. He caught the next one out, and fell into a dead sleep until it reached Osaka the next morning. It developed then that the plane he had seen had not been the *Asahi's*; that neither of the other teams had arrived yet; and that he had one of the first eyewitness accounts of the calamity. It made page one not only in the Osaka *Asahi* but, relayed by cable across Siberia, in many other papers all over the world.

IN SUMMER, on the east coast of Japan, the prevailing winds are usually off the sea by day and off the shore by night. Shifts of the wind during the first day of fire, though affected by the up-drafts created by the conflagration, had followed this general pattern. When the same shifts were repeated on Sunday, it brought the fire in the downtown area of Tokyo back across much of the ground that had already been burned over the day before. This, along with the demolition work of the fire department, contributed to the extinction of the flames by about 4 or 5 A.M. on Monday. In Yokohama, where the fires had started faster and had less ground to cover, the flames, except at the oil tanks, had died down on Sunday afternoon. Thereafter the problem that confronted the inhabitants of both cities was that of how to maintain existence in the ruins.

Of Tokyo's total population, about 100,000 had been burned to death or otherwise disposed of by the quake or the fire. More than 2,500,000, however, remained alive; and of these more than 1,500,-000, or about 60 per cent, were now completely homeless. In Yokohama, where there were nearly 500,000 survivors, conditions were proportionately worse. Among the homeless, a substantial number—perhaps 150,000 in Tokyo and 30,000 in Yokohama—were severely burned or otherwise injured. For such numbers, urban hospital facilities would have been hopelessly inadequate even if many of the hospitals had not been destroyed. And over and above the problem of caring for the injured was that of supplying shelter, not only for the injured but also for all the rest of the dispossessed; and of providing food, water and sanitation for the entire population.

Of these problems the most acute was perhaps that of sanitation, which was complicated by two factors. One was the absence of any dependable supply of water—especially of drinking water.

The other was the presence of the corpses—some piled up in open spaces, like the 40,000 at the Army Clothing Depot, others concealed in the ruins of burned-out houses. In the prevailing hot, clear weather—the first rain after the earthquake was a heavy shower on Monday night—these obviously needed to be got rid of as rapidly as possible, since they constituted a major health menace. With no transportation or other means of disposal available, it was hard to see how to go about the job.

Intensifying all these problems was the fact that, until Monday morning when Admiral Count Yamamoto's cabinet actually began to deal with them, responsibility for government belonged to the outgoing Cabinet, whose members had tendered their resignations and dispersed. At its emergency meeting on Sunday afternoon—while the Yamamoto Cabinet was being formed and later invested with authority by the Prince Regent on the lawn of the Akasaka Palace—the outgoing Cabinet, in addition to proclaiming martial law, took other steps which formed the basis for subsequent government procedure in the crisis. One of these was authorization of some ten million yen as a special Earthquake Relief Fund. Another was the establishment of an Emergency Relief Bureau —of which the Prime Minister and the Home Minister were to be President and Vice-president respectively.

The Emergency Relief Bureau, through which the Yamamoto Cabinet later did its best to cope with the emergency, was composed of eleven departments responsible for general affairs, food, shelter, materials, communication, water, hygiene and medicine, police, intelligence, donations, and accounting. In addition to the Prime and Home Ministers, officers of the Bureau were to include the Governor of Tokyo Prefecture, the Metropolitan Police Chief and several others. They would be assisted by a staff of some seven hundred workers, clerks and bureau chiefs. The Bureau got started on its job immediately.

One of the first and most urgent items of business was, inevitably, that of getting rid of the dead. In Tokyo, the sanitary department of the metropolitan police, in cooperation with the Relief Bureau, recruited thousands of workers among the homeless—and in most cases, of course, also jobless—refugees to recover the bodies of the drowned from the rivers and canals and to dig out those who had been crushed to death or burned from the ruins of buildings and houses. Each ward established a morgue in which identifiable bodies were held for two days to enable relatives to examine them. Records as to where each body was found included belongings found with it and, if feasible, a photograph. Mass crematoria were established at several conveniently central locations and the bodies carried there first by ox wagon and later by truck, as gasoline supplies became available and the streets were cleared of rubble.

For the firing of these crematoria, many thousands of tons of pine logs had to be brought into the city by hand. Wood fires proved adequate everywhere except at the Depot where, understandably, more effective methods were required. On September 8, a man named Hideo Katayama, the inventor of a new type of gasoline equipment for crematoria, offered his highly specialized services to the government. They were gratefully accepted and for several days thereafter gasoline was sprayed over the acres of dead bodies and kept burning constantly.

The immense problem of caring for the injured had begun to demand attention within an hour of the first shock—when the metropolitan police, finding its regular first-aid station menaced by the fire, had moved it to Hibiya Park, across the street from the Imperial Hotel. By 3:30 that afternoon, ten police department medical teams, each consisting of a doctor, a health officer, a clerk and a policeman, had been dispatched to various zones of the city. Teams Number Four and Five, assigned to the Clothing Depot area, reported that they were unable to reach their stations and were reassigned. Messengers were also dispatched to hospitals and to the medical schools of the universities to round up reinforcements. The results were disappointing; most of the institutions that were still in operation had no personnel to spare.

On September 2, the situation began to improve slightly, when a score or so of doctors arrived from medical schools and hospitals that had been burned out, while dozens of others made their way into the capital from surrounding suburbs. Drugs and medicines, requisitioned from drugstores and manufacturers, were distributed to the volunteers. By the Monday after the earthquake, some eighty medical teams were doing their best to care for the injured —for whom, of course, in most cases, only the sketchiest sort of improvised shelter could be provided. The number of medical teams increased through the next few days, as the Relief Bureau recruited further aid from other cities; meanwhile the number of patients decreased rapidly, chiefly through the death of thousands of the most severely injured.

While the medical teams were being organized, Army authorities brought some six regiments of soldiers into Tokyo to reinforce the resident garrison; by September 8, there were 35,000 troops in the area. While the engineers set about repairing roads and bridges, railroads, and telephone and telegraph lines, other troops brought in food and medical supplies both from the Army's own supplies and from civilian sources in other cities. Mobile kitchens were set up and operated; at the Imperial Palace Plaza, Ueno Park, and similar areas, rice was served around the clock to never-ending queues of refugees. Communications between Tokyo headquarters and Army units on the outskirts of the city or elsewhere were maintained by a force of some four hundred highly efficient carrier pigeons. The air force in Japan—as indicated by the training mission there of Major Chichester-Smith—was still something of a novelty, but the few planes available rendered valuable services. One of these was a flight from the capital to Nikko in order to drop documents reporting the disaster to Their Imperial Majesties along with the news that their son, the Prince Regent, had survived uninjured in the Akasaka Palace.

For the first three nights, the city was in total darkness—except for the glow provided by the conflagration which, on the first night, provided enough light to read by as far as ten miles from downtown Tokyo. On the fourth night after the earthquake, a few street-lamps were working again; by the fifth, electric service in a few public buildings and houses had been partially restored. Streetcar service, with free rides for the injured and reduced fares for all, started sporadically on September 5. The Tokyo Gas Company, whose broken mains had been a major contributing cause in the spread of the fire, soon got some of them mended and back into service. Within a week shops had begun to reopen in makeshift quarters on the ruined Ginza. On the morning of the quake, Miss Florence Wells, an American teacher in a mission school, had dropped in at Mitsukoshi to buy a dozen Mason jars, explaining to the clerk that she needed them delivered that very afternoon since the blueberry jam they were to contain was already cooking in a pot on her stove. Two weeks later, when she visited the reopened store, the same clerk waited on her and apologized for his failure to have the jars delivered. Miss Wells replied that this had caused her no inconvenience, since the earthquake had upset the jam pot.

Of all Tokyo's shortages the day after the quake, the most acute was naturally that of water. The few remaining private wells that contained reliable reserves were sought out by thirsty survivors who formed long queues beside them in areas where there were no other sources of supply. Laboring frantically through the night of September 1, workmen hooked up emergency pipe connections along the surface of the ground to restore service from the Yodo-bashi Reservoir, Tokyo's major source, to the few mains in the city that were still workable. By Sunday afternoon, there was a trickle of water at many of the city's hydrants. These were supplemented for the next several days by Army water carts which rationed out cupfuls as they were drawn slowly through the burned-out areas, where refugees ran after them to catch drops in their cupped hands.

The excitement of the earthquake had brought on numerous miscarriages and premature births—among the latter being the son of an American missionary couple named Martin who was later given the appropriate baptismal name of Jishin to commemorate the occasion. A special tent hospital was set up for such lyings-in, and later a municipal maternity home for pregnant but homeless women, of whom there were several hundred in urgent need of care. Temporary housing in the form of army tents and shacks made out of rubble sprang up in the refugee areas. Milk depots for children were established, and within an amazingly short time polished rice was on sale in the public markets. Tokyo's fishing fleet, substantially reduced by fire along the waterfront, resumed its activities and the catch was soon on sale in improvised stalls within a few blocks of the Ginza.

For the first two days after the earthquake, all traffic in and out of both Tokyo and Yokohama was on foot or by ox cart. Several weeks passed before the Tokaido line, operating between the two cities and to the cities south and west of them, could be repaired. Within two days of the earthquake, however, trains for the north were leaving from within Tokyo, packed inside and out by as many refugees as could squeeze into or clamber on to them. Within two weeks, officials estimated that there had been three million departures from the city, and over two million entries or re-entries. In the six weeks after the earthquake, Tokyo's population dropped from over two-and-a-half to one-and-a-half million.

Newspapers in the capital began to resume publication only on September 18, and then only in limited fashion. Meanwhile, the dearth of news in the capital was ingeniously, if by no means completely, rectified by students at the Imperial University.

Under the leadership of Professors Gentaro Suehiro and Juen Hozumi, who headed the Law Department, they set up an "Information Bureau on Quake Damage" which, advertising its existence in out-of-town papers on September 11, offered to provide correspondents with information about their relatives in the capital or to answer other questions relating to the catastrophe. Between September 15 and October 19, some 35,000 letters were handled by the three hundred or so students who served in the bureau; in addition to helping to reunite families, safeguard property and re-discover missing persons, the bureau compiled details of damage in various areas, which proved of considerable value to later investigating committees. One of their most important contributions was a list of missing children based on inquiries from orphanages and asylums as well as private homes. This facilitated both the return of waifs to their parents or guardians and the later disposition of those who could not be so returned among the special schools and orphanages eventually set up for them.

Meanwhile, although neither Tokyo nor Yokohama was aware of it, help had been on the way since the evening of the first day. Within hours of the time when the first news of the disaster was published in the United States, plans for relief on an unprec-edented scale were under way. Less than twenty-four hours after the quake—on the afternoon of September 1, by Washington time —President Calvin Coolidge, in his capacity as head of the Amer-ican Red Cross, called for a five-million-dollar relief program in which every major city had an appropriate quota to fulfill. Most gave far more than they were asked for—notably San Francisco, to which Japan had contributed $100,000 when conditions had been reversed in 1906. Now, with a chance to reciprocate, San Francisco did so in heartwarming style, raising five times that amount.

Long before these funds could be translated into the tangible supplies that they later provided, a more immediate form of succor was on its way from comparatively near at hand. At the time of the earthquake, the United States Asiatic Fleet was stationed at Dairen, Manchuria—now Talien, Red China—and its commanding officer, Admiral Edwin A. Anderson, received the call for help sent from the *Korea Maru* by Police Chief Morioka on the evening of September 1. Loading all the available supplies that night, and summoning other United States ships from other ports as far distant as Manila, Admiral Anderson, in his flagship the *Huron,* got under way for Yokohama so fast that he arrived there less than forty-eight hours later, when the ruins were still smoking and oil was still burning in the harbor. On the way, he passed some elements of the Japanese fleet proceeding in the opposite direction. It developed that, prior to the earthquake, they had received orders to execute routine maneuvers and, in the absence of official cancellation from headquarters in Tokyo, were proceeding to obey them.

This was by no means the only example of incongruous response to catastrophe provided by the Japanese Navy. An even more dramatic one was afforded by the Admiral in charge of the port of Tokyo who ordered the captain of an American destroyer to take his vessel out of the harbor since it was not officially open to foreigners. The idea that the United States or some other Western power might take advantage of the disaster to launch an invasion was, however, perhaps less shocking as an example of bureaucratic rigidity on the part of the Japanese than as evidence of the poor opinion of Western integrity justified by the West's own previous conduct in the Far East. The help given by the United States in general and by the United States fleet in particular, did much to alter this opinion, at least temporarily.

In both Tokyo—where the order of the Japanese Admiral was disregarded—and Yokohama, the actions of the United States fleet were a major element in relief. In the harbor at Yokohama a freighter loaded with Ford trucks was promptly commandeered. For weeks thereafter these trucks, and later on shipments of others like them, most of which were put to use as buses, became the principal means of transportation in both cities. Meanwhile, in Yokohama the marines went ashore to clear debris, build pontoon docks, and set up a tent-city for refugees. The fleet stayed on for ten days until Red Cross ships began to arrive. When Admiral Anderson departed, all suspicion and hostility had long since vanished, and he received an accolade from his Japanese opposite number: "You Americans . . . have created a miracle."

AT THE IMPERIAL HOTEL, still completely in his element the day after the earthquake, Tetsuzo Inumaru said to his kitchen staff, "Don't try to save any food. We have enough on hand for today. Use it all up, and tomorrow I will find some more." On Monday morning, Inumaru was faced by the need of ready cash with which to justify this promise; since it was the beginning of the month, receipts for the previous one had already been banked and there were no new ones on hand.

The fact that no banks were open did not deter Inumaru more than momentarily. He went to the Foreign Office, explained the importance of taking proper care of his international visitors and got what he needed. Thus equipped, he dispatched the hotel's vehicles, including a Cadillac touring car which Frank Lloyd Wright had left behind, into the country north of the city where the roads were still passable, to search for provisions. They came back with enough to keep things going for a day or two. Inumaru used some of the supplies for his guests and some in a soup kitchen for refugees, which he set up across the street in Hibiya Park.

Of the major embassies in Tokyo, the American, Brazilian, French and Italian had been burned to the ground and the British badly damaged. Inumaru invited the heads of these missions to make use of the Imperial for combined living quarters and office space. The British were assigned a balcony over the lobby. The

Americans had the north wing, and the American Relief Commission, when it arrived from Manila a few days later, was installed in the ground-floor grillroom with storage facilities in the rear. The banquet hall and the promenade leading to it were turned over to the Tokyo newspapers, as they got their presses reorganized and prepared to resume publication. The south wing was handed over to the public utilities that had been burned out. Many of these organizations brought their own supplies; staff members camped in the lobbies and cooked caldrons of rice on open campfires in the parking area beside the front driveway.

Knowing that the residence of Baron Okura was in the path of the fire, Inumaru had paid a call on the old peer at dawn on Monday morning, even before his visit to the Foreign Office. He found the Baron, wearing kimono and a nightcap, standing on the lawn near the ashes of what had been his villa, watching the smoldering embers of his private museum. This had housed an art collection valued at a hundred million yen, the assembling of which had been the major interest of his life. One of Inumaru's conversational mannerisms was, and is, to jab a listener gently with his forefinger in order to ensure full attention. Of this meeting with the Baron, he later said, "I patted him and talked to him and persuaded him to come away with me." Downtown, the Baron inspected the ruins of the building that had housed his offices and then came to the Imperial where Inumaru gave him a dish of porridge for breakfast and got him installed in a comfortable room.

In the excitement of the crowded days that followed, one small incident made so little impression on Inumaru that he failed to mention it in his own memoirs of the period. This was an exchange of cables with the United States, which started soon after the cable office opened for limited service on September 6. In the United States, Frank Lloyd Wright, just then engaged on a project in Los Angeles, had been following the earthquake stories with even closer attention than most other newspaper readers. On

September 4, among the rumors from Tokyo published in the
United States and elsewhere was one to the effect that the Imperial
Hotel had been totally destroyed. When Los Angeles *Examiner*
reporters called Wright to get his comment, Wright expressed in-
credulity and dashed off a cable of inquiry which eventually reached
Inumaru. Inumaru took it to Baron Okura and helped him compose
the reply:

HOTEL STANDS UNDAMAGED AS MONUMENT OF YOUR GENIUS HUNDREDS
OF HOMELESS PROVIDED BY PERFECTLY MAINTAINED SERVICE CONGRAT-
ULATIONS OKURA

The cable from Baron Okura, which reached Wright in Wiscon-
sin on September 13, was more than a mere testimonial. Under
the circumstances, it was also an eyewitness comment on the earthquake by a distinguished member of the Japanese peerage, and one
of the very few bits of cheerful news that had come out of the
disaster area. When Wright—never noted for reticence in such
matters—released the story to the press, it understandably made
front-page news all over the world. Thus it created the legend—
apparently almost as imperishable as it is erroneous—that the
Imperial Hotel was the only building in Tokyo that had withstood
the earthquake. This legend in turn provided a cornerstone for
Wright's worldwide reputation and possibly did more than anything
else to popularize the school of architecture which he represented
—and which, in the next four decades, was to revolutionize the
appearance of most of the great cities of the world.

It is quite true that the Imperial Hotel did stand up through the
earthquake with no damage more serious than a slight buckling
here and there, thus justifying most of Wright's hopes and claims
for it. It is equally true that 99 per cent of all other buildings in
Tokyo, including most of the major ones in the downtown area as
well as many hundreds of thousands of the city's flimsiest wooden
shacks, also stood up through the earthquake—as distinct from the

ensuing fire—just as well if not better. If the ability to design earthquake-resistant structures were to be accepted as the appropriate criterion, the hero of the occasion was not so much Wright as an eminent British architect named Josiah Conder, who received no accolade whatsoever.

Josiah Conder, who had died three years before the earthquake, had come to Japan in 1882 at the age of thirty to work in the Home Ministry of the highly cosmopolitan Meiji government. He married a Japanese wife and stayed in Tokyo thereafter with only two trips home to his native London in the course of the next forty-eight years. In 1891, the severe Mino-Owari earthquake, which at least equalled the Kanto one in magnitude and affected a wider, though far less populous, region, made a profound impression upon Conder. When called upon soon afterward to design the first of a series of downtown office buildings for the Mitsubishi companies, Conder chose a style which might be called Bloomsbury pillbox, as opposed to Wright's avant-garde Aztec, but he left nothing to chance so far as seismic menace was concerned.

Conder's way of dealing with the menace differed radically from Wright's. It was simply to make the walls out of brick a yard thick and so heavily reinforced by steel rods and sheets of corrugated iron that even today they defy the efforts of up-to-date wrecking machines attempting to tear them down to make room for modern replacements. Not only did Conder's original Mitsubishi building stand up undamaged through both quake and fire but so did a dozen or so more or less exact copies put up by his disciples, all of which were four stories high to the Imperial's three, not to mention numerous other Conder structures elsewhere in the area. If Conder has been largely forgotten by the rest of the world, he is still appropriately revered in Tokyo where his statue, that of a slender dignified gentleman with a drooping mustache, stands on the campus of what is now called Tokyo University, and where his work on Japanese landscape gardening, still obtainable in the rare-book stores of the Kanda district, is rightly regarded as a classic.

While Inumaru was turning the Imperial into a sort of preview of the United Nations and making its lobbies the center of Tokyo's post-earthquake diplomatic, journalistic and industrial revival, things in the Honjo area of town were going forward somewhat differently. There, on his way back toward the Sumida River from his visit to his dead wife and dead children, where he had left the stick with the card across their bodies, Dr. Ikeguchi saw a riderless horse standing in the road. It occurred to him that he could perhaps ride this horse to the house in the suburbs where his wife's family lived to tell them what had happened. He tried to clamber onto the animal's back but with his burned hands it was difficult. Presently a man who was watching called to him there was no use in the attempt; the horse was severely injured and could not move.

A Red Cross ambulance came by and offered to take the doctor to a hospital, but he refused, saying that he was on his way to find someone to care for the bodies of his family. He wandered about and presently came to a fruit-storage shed beside the river, which had somehow remained partly intact. The owner of the shed recognized him and said that he could enter and lie down. The doctor lay down on the floor of the shed and stayed there. Around him were other people suffering from injuries and severe burns. One by one they died and others took their places but the doctor went on living. Medical relief teams came to treat the sufferers from time to time. The doctor noticed that they held handkerchiefs over their noses while they were in the shed.

One day when a young doctor from one of the teams was standing near where he was lying, Doctor Ikeguchi tugged at the bottom of his white medical robe to attract his attention and asked him for a heart injection. The doctor knelt to insert the needle and, in searching for a clean place on his charred muddy skin, turned back the sleeve of his shirt. In doing so he noticed the doctor's cuff links, a present from the Yasudas, which were platinum with a diamond in the middle. Judging from this that he was a man of means, the young doctor asked who he was, and on hearing that he was a doctor also, went out to get him a glass of medicinal wine. When he returned, Dr. Ikeguchi informed the young doctor of his need to get to the house of his wife's family to tell them about the bodies. He asked the young doctor to come back with a car if he could find one. The young doctor promised to do so if he could. He did not reappear.

Two days after that, his sixth in the shed, when Dr. Ikeguchi had given up all hope of ever seeing the half-promised car, the owner of the shed came in and told him it was there. Refusing a stretcher, Dr. Ikeguchi got slowly to his feet. He shook maggots off his hands. Others fell from his face. He walked to the car, got in, and gave the driver the directions.

CHAPTER VIII

. . . YA-OKI

EIGHT TIMES GET UP

ACCORDING TO the best available estimates—those compiled after many months of research by Professor Imamura and released in 1925—human casualties attributable to the Great Kanto Earthquake were: dead, 99,331; missing, 43,476; injured, 103,733. Assuming that most of those who were missing never reappeared and also that some of those seriously injured later died of their injuries, the total number of deaths must have been well over 140,000, which is the round figure generally accepted.

While the loss of life involved was in itself enough to qualify the Kanto Dai-shinsai as the most terrible natural calamity in history, other statistics provide confirmation. In Tokyo alone, for example, the total area covered by the fire amounted to some 4,500 acres, or nearly seven square miles—not quite twice the area covered by the great London, Chicago and San Francisco fires put together.

Of the city's 500,000 houses, over 300,000 were burned down. More than half of these were residences, but the ruins also included, using round numbers, 3,000 government buildings, 1,500 schools and libraries, 2,500 temples, shrines and churches, 5,000 banks and office buildings, 20,000 factories and warehouses and 250 theaters and amusement centers. Not included in the latter figures was the entire Yoshiwara licensed quarter which—much to the horror of reform elements in the capital and elsewhere—was one of the first parts of the city to be rebuilt and restored to its previous prosperity.

Though no Europeans died in Tokyo, the damage to the embassies had interesting sequels, one of which was recalled recently by a well-known United States businessman in Tokyo named Frederick C. Taylor. Then a young representative for an export firm, Taylor lived in Room 114 at the Imperial, where one of his friends was the attaché who happened to be duty officer at the United States Embassy on September 1. At the time of the earthquake, Taylor had been in a rickshaw hurrying to cash a check at his bank before it closed at noon. The quake caused the rickshaw man to drop the shafts and run; Taylor made his way on foot to the Imperial, stopping en route to help rescue two dozen or so of the hundred people who had been trapped inside the Mitsui Club when its roof collapsed, before the rest burned to death. In the afternoon it became obvious that the old-fashioned wooden colonial building that housed the United States Chancery and the residence of the Ambassador, who had left town for the Labor Day weekend, was in the path of the fire. Taylor, the duty officer, and some others spent several hours removing part of its contents to caves in a nearby embankment prepared by the gardeners.

When the building burned to the ground the next day, all that remained was a fireproof brick vault under the northeast corner, which had been used for storing confidential embassy files. While the vault survived the fire, the ruins disclosed a detail of the foundation that had theretofore escaped the attention of the vault's custodians. This was an underground passage leading from outside the embassy into one corner of the vault, where its entrance was concealed by stacks of papers. Who had built the passage remained a mystery, as did the questions of who had been using it and for how long.

Among the magnificent private art collections consumed by the flames, Baron Okura's museum was perhaps the most celebrated, but there were dozens of others of comparable value. These included innumerable paintings, scrolls, picture rolls, screens, woodblock prints, theatrical masks, ceramics, and furnishings of all sorts, as well as such examples of various peculiarly Japanese specialties as Prince Isaburo Yamagata's sword collection, including the enormous antique blade known as Ichimonji, once the property of the Tokogawa family; an historic teacup owned by Count Matsudaira, which had been made by the potter Choshiro for Rikyu, the originator of the tea ceremony; and a collection of ancient toys owned by Yonekichi Namba, along with 5,000 books on this recondite subject. Among the burned libraries, which included the Ohashi collection of 90,000 books, a large portion of them rare, and the libraries of the Departments of Commerce and Finance of 400,000 to 500,000 volumes each, the greatest single loss was the library of the Imperial University, comprising some 700,000 items, many of them irreplaceable.

In Yokohama, the destruction was proportionately greater than Tokyo's. There, about three square miles, or half the city's total area, were so completely burned out that the hollow shells of less than half a dozen buildings were all that remained standing. The burned area included Yokohama's most important commercial, and most desirable residential, sections—the equivalents of which, in Tokyo, remained largely undestroyed. In round numbers, 60,000 of the city's 100,000 buildings burned to the ground; and this figure did not include 20,000 others which had been wholly or partially destroyed by the quake. The percentage of destruction from both sources was thus roughly 80 as compared to Tokyo's 60. Over a thousand boats, sampans, barges and miscellaneous river or

149

harbor craft were burned in Yokohama, compared to less than half that many in Tokyo; and in Yokohama, the wharf area and harbor facilities, which were the port's main reason for existence, were destroyed totally.

Damage in the smaller towns and cities along the coast—Yokosuka, Kamakura, Odawara, Atami and Ito, whether by earthquake, fire, tsunami or combinations of the three—varied from 90 per cent in Odawara to 20 per cent in Ito, where tsunami had prevented a destructive fire. Mountain towns and villages, especially Hakone and Miyanoshita, suffered severely. Substantial tracts of forest timber and farmland were destroyed or made unusable throughout the area.

Estimates of the total value of the property destroyed were necessarily rough approximations. These ranged from a low of half a billion yen, or some $250 million, proposed by a conservative British appraiser, to a high of ten billion yen, or $5 billion, set by Japan's Treasury Department. The official report of the Japanese Home Office, compiled under Viscount Goto and Rentaro Mizuno —who, in a later Cabinet, resumed his former post—puts the figure rather reasonably at five billion yen or $2.5 billion. This is based on a modest evaluation of 45 yen per square yard for frame buildings, 75 for stone or brick, and 95 for concrete or ferroconcrete, with 60 per cent of these values allowed for partial destruction and 30 per cent for serious damage. Interior appointments were valued on a sliding scale, from a low of 1,200 yen to a high of 2,500.

Doubts as to the accuracy of this figure have been raised on the ground that it represents some 7 per cent of Japan's entire national wealth as estimated by the *Japan Year Book* of 1923. However, the error here may well lie in an undervaluation of the national wealth; and in any case, none of the earthquake-damage figures make any allowance for the damage to the nation's economy in general, let alone for the loss of human life.

Destruction of life and property were of course, technically speaking, among the more superficial consequences of the earth-quake. Its subterranean and submarine effects were also noteworthy and made profound changes in the topography of the Kanto area, which were revealed two years later by the Land Survey Department of the Japanese Army.

According to the researches of the Army engineers, the land in three distinct parts of the earthquake region, taking an arbitrary point in Tokyo as the standard, was elevated to considerable distances. One of these was the region east and north of Sagami Bay, where it rose as much as six and a half feet; another was the Boso Peninsula, east of Tokyo Bay, in which some portions rose the same amount; a third was the mountainous region west of Yokohama, where a rise of seven and a half feet, highest in the whole earthquake area, was recorded. In other parts of the earth-quake region, chiefly a strip to the northwest of Yokohama, there were depressions reaching a maximum of five and a half feet. Most of these changes made no particular difference to the inhabitants except at a few points along the coast where harbor installations at elevated portions of the beaches had to be rebuilt nearer the water and where the residents were annoyed for some months by a low-tide smell, coming from previously submerged land which had been exposed to the air.

In view of the rather modest measurements of the changes on dry land, what seemed to have happened to the floor of Sagami was, to say the least, astonishing. According to a survey made soon after the quake, parts of the bay floor were apparently raised as much as 800 feet while other parts were depressed by as much as 1,500. These results, shown by soundings taken immediately after the earthquake, seemed so improbable that a much more detailed survey was undertaken lasting from late September, 1923, until the following January. This, however, seemed to confirm the earlier one. Since it would appear unlikely that the whole bottom of Sagami Bay could have been in such a state of violent agitation without causing much larger tsunami than those actually observed, various theories have been advanced to account for the discrepancy.

One of these theories, and possibly the most tenable, is that a large part of the dramatic change in the soundings was attributable to underwater landslides rather than to a general alteration in the submarine topography. The bottom of the bay, of which some parts are as much as a thousand fathoms deep, is thoroughly irregular and marked by many cliffs, canyons and miscellaneous declivities. If the face of a cliff slid away, the result would be a marked increase of depth where the face had been and a marked decrease at the cliff's base. Thus a very few landslides on the scale of the supramarine one at Nebukawa might account for vast alterations in soundings made from the surface.

The trouble with the otherwise highly plausible landslide theory is that, if it were correct, the changes in soundings would follow a more or less discernible pattern and would not affect wide areas. Since neither circumstance can be clearly deduced from the evidence, other tentative explanations have also been put forward. One is that the original soundings—taken when there was no reason to be precisely accurate about either the depth of the water or the position of the boat whence the line was dropped—may well have been in error. Another is that while the sea bottom may have changed as dramatically as the soundings show, the changes may have been gradual and a contributing cause, rather than a result, of the earthquake. Seismologists are still arguing about these matters and likely to go on doing so.

Further controversy about causes and consequences of the earthquake concern the fault lines discovered after it. Some fifteen major faults were traced at different parts of the region, varying in length from twelve and a half miles to six-tenths of a mile and, in vertical displacement, from six and a half feet to eight inches. Whether these caused, or were caused by, the quake is a moot point,

as is the matter of which faults related to the main shock and which
to the aftershocks.

While many missing people were, as usual in such disasters,
rumored to have been swallowed up in fissures, there were, also
as usual, no authenticated instances of such mishaps. There were,
however, plenty of fissures, especially around Yokohama and Sagami Bay where the proximity to the epicenter and the nature of
the soil facilitated such developments. A good many of these
occurred along main roadways and—in the form of landslides—
along the banks of rivers and canals. Among many major landslides,
the most spectacular were Nebukawa's, which on further investigation were found to consist of two separate disturbances. One was
a landslide wherein three million cubic yards of a loamy mountain-
side fell a distance of 650 feet into a valley. Another was the
subsequent mudflow, 250 yards wide and 50 feet deep, that obliter-
ated Nebukawa village and discolored Sagami Bay for six miles off
the shore.

After the earthquake was over, people began recalling instances
of strange behavior on the part of Japan's famous hot springs and
geysers, which, in retrospect, seemed to have been advance indications that something strange was going on underground. In some
cases the springs were muddy before the shock; in other cases they
were hotter than usual. After the earthquake, similar malfunction-
ings were noted, especially at Atami where one celebrated geyser
began boiling more vigorously and on a new schedule, while other
hot springs got hotter or increased their output. Possibly the most
dramatic of all the after-effects was a *yamatsunami*, or mountain-
earthquake wave, which occurred near the village of Oyama-machi.
Here a heavy rain which fell on September 15 infiltrated many of
the cracks and fissures that the quake had opened in the mountain.
The result was a landslide in which an acre or so of forest descended
on the town, destroying its 140 houses, which all the inhabitants,
suspecting what was about to happen, had sensibly vacated.

Of all the effects of the earthquake on the conformation of the ground in the earthquake area, the oddest was perhaps that which occurred near the village of Chigasaki in a rice field bordering the Sagami River. Here after the quake a double row of seven wooden pillars, each about two feet thick, was found standing three feet or so above the surface of the ground. They looked like the pillars of a bridge, and research indicated that that was exactly what they were. The bridge was one which, according to ancient records, had been built in 1182.

The effects of the quake upon the floor of Tokyo Bay had unexpected consequences. Before it took place, municipal authorities in Yokohama had been considering a plan to deepen the harbor close to shore so that more big liners could moor along the jetties. After the earthquake, it was found that the harbor had been deepened enough to obviate the need for this project. Rubble from ruined buildings provided fill for a fine park, which now extends half a mile long and fifty yards wide along the seaward side of what used to be the waterfront.

To PEOPLE WHO LIVE in areas of the world that are untroubled by earthquakes, volcanoes or typhoons, a question that sometimes arises about those who are exposed to such hazards is "Why don't they move elsewhere?" After the Kanto Dai-shinsai a few people in Tokyo began to ask this question of themselves and speedily found the answer to it. Tokyo was central not only to the Japanese archipelago as a whole but also to its largest fertile plain and major area of food production. Moreover, even after the disaster, a million or so people were still in fairly comfortable residence there; and there was nowhere else that promised to be much more secure. In short, if Japan was to go on being inhabited at all, Tokyo remained the right place for the capital.

For rebuilding Yokohama most of the same reasons could be invoked, with one additional one. This was that Tokyo needed a port, and hence, if the capital was to be rebuilt, it followed that Yokohama must be rebuilt also. Yokohama's merchants began installing temporary warehouses before the ruins had stopped smoking. The first shipment of silk to leave the port was loaded on September 18.

Plans for the reconstruction of Tokyo had likewise begun before the city ceased burning. Investiture by the Prince Regent of the Yamamoto Cabinet took place by candlelight in the tea house of the Akasaka Palace—since the Imperial Palace was not regarded as altogether safe—on the later afternoon of September 2. As the plans for rebuilding went forward thereafter, a new figure became increasingly important in them. This was the somewhat incongruous one of the historian Charles A. Beard, renowned in his native land chiefly as the co-author, with his wife Mary, of their widely admired *The Rise of American Civilization.*

The link which connected Beard, a rebel among scholars, with the renascence of Japanese civilization after the Kanto earthquake was reminiscent of that which had connected Wright, a rebel among architects, with the rise of the Imperial Hotel. Both consisted of personal contacts somewhat unpredictably established on Manhattan Island where the main difference was that, in Beard's case, the link was forged not on 57th Street but on 23rd, the site of Cooper Union. There, during the winter of 1920, a young Japanese government official named Yusuke Tsurumi attended the New School for Social Research at which Beard was giving a series of lectures. The following January, Tsurumi received a cable from his father-in-law in Tokyo asking him to send a report on how the major American cities had rid themselves of corruption in city government. Tsurumi paid a call upon Beard, who promptly directed him to the New York Institute of Municipal Research of which he was the president.

The father-in-law of Yusuke Tsurumi was none other than Viscount Shimpei Goto, who, after a distinguished career in industrial management, had then just entered the arena of public affairs as Mayor of Tokyo. Why Mayor Goto assumed that New York, at the dawn of the Mayor Walker era, was the place to do research on how to get rid of corruption rather than the reverse is a question that remains unanswered. However, among Viscount Goto's numerous personal idiosyncrasies, as his son-in-law was well aware, was a passion for all sorts of organizations but especially for organizations concerned with research. Characteristically, as soon as he received his son-in-law's report, he became entranced by the source of the material and determined that Tokyo should have something like it just as soon as possible. The Tokyo Institute for Municipal Research was launched in February, 1922, with funds supplied by the Yasuda family. In March, Viscount Goto had another inspiration. This was to ask his son-in-law to invite Professor Beard to visit Tokyo as the Tokyo Institute's first managing director. Professor Beard accepted promptly and promised to arrive with his family the following autumn.

Beard's first arrival in Tokyo took place on September 14, 1922. Mayor Goto, wearing a morning coat, met him at Tokyo Station and accompanied him to the then still unfinished Imperial Hotel. En route they conversed in German, which Tsurumi had informed each of them would be the most convenient common language. Beard's visit lasted six months, during which he visited all Japan's major cities and met most of the nation's leading dignitaries. It resulted in two substantial reports, of which the second, *Tokyo City Politics,* was later published in the United States by Macmillan. Beard refused remuneration in the form of money or medals; instead, he generously contributed two thousand yen to establish an annual prize for the best thesis on municipal affairs, to be awarded by the Mayor of Tokyo on Beard's birthday, June 4.

In inviting a distinguished American literary figure to head the Tokyo Institute for Municipal Research, Mayor Goto was demonstrating his shrewd insight into the then little-known science of what is now called motivational research. This insight caused him to suspect that such a novel subject as city planning might be more effectively introduced to his compatriots by an alien prophet than by a homegrown one. Just as both the Okuras were soon on first-name terms with their architect, Mayor Goto and his son-in-law hit it off well with their professor. The earthquake had been instrumental in persuading Goto to accept the portfolio of Internal Affairs, both because the rebuilding of Tokyo was clearly an enterprise in which his Institute could play a major role, and because it would provide an opportunity for renewing his association with Professor Beard. Goto's cable to Beard, drafted by Tsurumi and dated September 12, read as follows:

EARTHQUAKE FIRE DESTROYED GREATER PART TOKYO THOROUGHGOING RECONSTRUCTION NEEDED PLEASE COME IMMEDIATELY IF POSSIBLE EVEN FOR SHORT TIME.

Beard's reply was admirably specific:

LAY OUT NEW STREETS FORBID BUILDING WITHOUT STREET LINES UNIFY RAILWAY STATION.

This time, when Beard arrived on October 6, Tsurumi and a party of distinguished citizens went out on a launch to meet his ship at Yokohama. After inspecting the ruins of that city, the professor and his wife drove on to Tokyo where they put up at the Imperial. Beard stayed for six weeks during which he and Viscount Goto had time to devise plans for rebuilding Tokyo in a style calculated to make it one of the world's most beautiful, and certainly its most up-to-date, capital. The gist of this scheme was set forth by Beard in a "Memorandum Relative to the Reconstruction of Tokyo," which he presented to his host before leaving. Had the plan been executed, it might have saved a hundred thousand or so lives in the next unfolding of the Flowers of Edo—which took place, some-

157

what ahead of traditional schedule, in the form of the fire-bomb raid of March, 1945.

The problem of rebuilding the great cities of the Kanto Plain in general and Tokyo in particular was undeniably a tremendous one. However, in confronting it, Viscount Goto had several substantial assets in addition to Professor Beard. One of these was the paradoxically stimulating and even cheering effect which history shows that great catastrophes are likely to have upon that portion of the population which survives them.

Just what causes this oft-noted reaction to large-scale death and destruction remains something of a puzzle. Observers of kindly disposition ascribe it to the innate generosity of human nature whereby, in time of trouble, people seize the chance to show their love for their fellow men. Less gracious commentators explain the phenomenon on different grounds. They argue that what survivors feel is primarily a selfish satisfaction in having remained alive—a satisfaction which guilt and vanity then conspire to intensify by ascribing the survival to virtue, acumen or the direct intervention of some deity. Secondarily, the euphoria thus occasioned may be further intensified by the realization that, in addition to being far better off than the dead victims, they are now, despite their own wounds or losses, better off than many of their fellow survivors, whose sufferings have been even more severe.

Finally, since man associates any improvement of his own status with violent and destructive revolution, violence and destruction—even when they result from natural causes—may, by Pavlovian reasoning, convince him that a revolution must have taken place and his estate have been accordingly elevated. Nor is this conclusion, although ill-founded, wholly erroneous; for disaster does to some degree mean a fresh start for everyone; and for the vast majority, a fresh start implies an unexpected, and encouraging, competitive gain.

Whatever view one takes as to the underlying motivation, witnesses to Japan's response to the earthquake agree that it constituted an unprecedented display of human resilience to misfortune. Typical was the experience of a traveler who, obliged to journey from Hakone to Yokohama on foot the day after the earthquake, found that the already unrivaled manners of the Japanese had been, if anything, improved. When he stopped at a small shop for tea and cakes, the shopkeeper refused to let him pay for his repast. She said the tea was always gratis and that, on this particular day, she was giving away cakes as well.

Kindness and consideration were by no means confined to the poor. Out of his privy purse, the Prince Regent contributed ten million yen, or the equivalent of the government's Emergency Fund, on the day after the disaster. Other areas of Japan sent not only personnel and food but substantial gifts of clothing and cash. Individual contributions of all sorts poured in from benefactors of every description to assist the government in its efforts to deal with the relief problem. Characteristic was the action of a manufacturer of soya bean sauce near Tokyo, who converted his factory into a relief kitchen from which rice, pickles and drinking water were sent downriver to the capital by motorboat—as a means, he explained, of expressing his gratitude for patronage in the past.

Ever since the San Francisco earthquake-fire of 1906, when some insurance companies paid claims in full and many others refused to do so, underwriters had been wary about claims consequent upon such calamities. All Japanese policies carried an earthquake-exemption clause—although by no means all policyholders were aware of it; one of the few buildings in the whole area not so exempted was the Yokohama United Club, which was covered by Lloyd's of London. In the absence of legal claims against the insurance companies —all of which, of course, would have gone bankrupt if such claims had been valid—the Japanese government took the view that there was a moral obligation for the companies to pay what they could. Arrangements were promptly made whereby government loans en-

abled insurance companies to make "sympathy payments" of some
10 per cent of the face value of their policies. Knowledge that they
were entitled to such payments helped businessmen and householders to accept their losses with equanimity.

Assistance to the sufferers was by no means confined to domestic
sources; and the promptness of President Coolidge's appeal and
Admiral Anderson's dash from Dairen set patterns for many other
lands. Not long after the *Huron* paced the Asiatic fleet to
Yokohama, Britain's Asiatic squadron arrived, led by its flagship
Hawkins. French and Italian vessels presently joined them. Mon-
etary contributions poured in from Britain (four million yen),
China (a million and a half), Holland (three hundred thousand),
and many others including France, Italy, Belgium, Sweden,
Mexico and even little Siam. Several countries also made substantial contributions in kind, like the mobile hospitals worth some two
million yen sent by the French Press Association. Japanese residents
abroad sent home another million.

Most niggardly of the foreign contributions was that of the
U.S.S.R., consisting of a grandiose offer of medical aid—with
political strings attached which made it unacceptable. The biggest
was appropriately that of the United States, where the $5 million
called for by President Coolidge was duly oversubscribed by more
than 100 per cent. Total contributions from the United States and
her possessions amounted to 25 million yen, which, largely
converted into lumber, food, tents, blankets, medicine and other
essential supplies, began to arrive by the middle of the month.
Transports from the Philippines brought the commanding general
of the United States garrison and enough equipment to set up field
hospitals in Tokyo, Yokohama, and Kobe.

The flood of relief from abroad had a noteworthy effect upon
Japan's relations with the donor countries, especially the United
States. Only less precious than the gifts themselves were the sponta-
neous expressions of sympathy that accompanied them. Japan's

newspapers told how girls in San Francisco—citadel of the Hearst newspaper chain and its campaign against the "yellow peril"— raised funds for aid by selling bunches of flowers in the street to eager purchasers at $10 each; how the American Silk Association raised $150,000 in half an hour and then voted to add $250,000 more; and how a single family, the Rockefellers, contributed $200,000. They quoted an editorial from Hearst's San Francisco *Examiner* which said:

In the face of such appalling acts of nature, the sense of racial distinction sinks into insignificance. The people of San Francisco, rich and poor, should alike contribute to the relief of the Japanese.

Wide approval greeted United States Secretary of State Charles Evans Hughes's comment:

The traditional friendship between Japan and the United States has been further strengthened. . . . In the face of the present great misfortune to Japan, it is our universal desire to extend every relief. . . .

Japan's response was, as might have been expected, one of heartfelt gratitude, frequently and variously reiterated. At a mass meeting in Tokyo on Armistice Day, Chairman Raita Fujiyama of the Tokyo Chamber of Commerce read a resolution of thanks, which—adopted to thunderous applause and three banzais—was then sent to various donor countries. Thanks were offered by the Prince Regent at a joint meeting of the Diet. Prime Minister Yamamoto spoke from the nation's heart when he said:

The genuine friendship of the United States government and people demonstrated towards us at the time of our sorrow and distress will, I am firmly convinced, increase the intimacy of the two peoples and eventually further strengthen the links of the world's peace.

In Tokyo, a United States missionary encountered an old man reading one of the news posters which preceded full publication of daily editions of the newspapers. The poster contained news of recent shipments of United States relief; the old man said with tears in his eyes, "We always thought you scorned and hated us, but now we see that you really do not."

That Japan's government should have been in the process of change at the moment of the earthquake began to seem to have been a blessing in disguise. A new Cabinet, especially one including such a specialist in municipal government as Home Minister Goto, was surely just what was needed for the great work at hand. It appeared that the nation, as a sort of compensation for its dreadful suffering, could now expect better understanding on the part of the outside world and indeed perhaps a new era in East-West relations generally. The far-seeing Professor Beard, in the conclusion of his "Memorandum," struck the keynote when he said, "The drama of history is shifting from the Atlantic Ocean to the Pacific. Japan will play a great role in that drama and Tokyo will be the seat of many impressive scenes. . . ."

That the details of the scenes and the nature of the drama differed markedly from those anticipated by the great historian was perhaps only to be expected. Numerous tensions and stresses, whose consequences not even the most expert of social seismologists could have predicted, were at work beneath the surface of world society. Meanwhile, Tokyo, Yokohama and the other cities of the Kanto Plain began to throw themselves wholeheartedly, and even happily, into the great tasks of reconstruction.

IN YOKOHAMA the day after the earthquake, Antonios Pappa-dopoulos took stock of his situation. He had thirty-six yen, his revolver, his cello, his defective camera and the unimpaired use of all his faculties. Unlike most of the surviving Japanese residents of the city, few of the foreigners had friends or relatives elsewhere in Japan to whom they could turn for help. Unlike most of the foreign residents, Pappadopoulos could not even expect logistic support from overseas; his father, ruined in the Russian Revolution, was still in Odessa but now dependent on him rather than the other way around. Even the wily Ulysses, whose travels held the previous record for natural and supernatural hazards, had never encountered anything quite as monstrous as the world's worst earthquake. In the intervals of the hideous commotions that disturbed his encampment on Sunday night, Pappadopoulos gave thought to the same problem that had so often beset his renowned prototype: what to do next. On Monday morning, he proceeded to the waterfront to take action.

On the waterfront, the surviving European consuls—Consul Paul deJardin of France and several members of the British Mission had been burned to death, as well as United States Consul Max Kirjassof—had decided to evacuate their nationals as rapidly as possible. Pappadopoulos was given a choice of boarding either of two ships. One was the *City of Spokane,* which had just arrived with a shipment of six thousand tons of flour, diverted from Kobe by request from Washington, and which was returning to Seattle the next day. The other was the *Empress of Canada,* sister ship to the *Empress of Australia,* which had brought relief stores into port the afternoon before and was now about to sail for Kobe with some five hundred refugees. Pappadopoulos had half an hour in which to make up his mind. His wife favored Seattle and a new life in the United States, but he decided otherwise. The family boarded the *Empress of Canada* and disembarked at Kobe early on Wednesday.

What had most influenced Pappadopoulos in his decision to take the *Empress* to Kobe rather than the *City of Spokane* to Seattle was that he had at last devised a way in which, making a virtue of necessity, he could use the earthquake to solve the dilemma of what to do about his defective movie camera. His idea was that in Kobe he could borrow some money, buy some film and come back to

Yokohama on a relief ship to photograph the ruins. En route he could fix the camera; and the film would bring in enough to enable him to get a new start in business. Meanwhile, his family could wait for him in Kobe.

Things in the beginning worked out much as he had planned. In Kobe, he had no difficulty in borrowing two hundred and fifty yen with which he bought five cans of film containing two hundred feet each. A relief ship, the *West O'Rowa*, was leaving for Yokohama that same night, and Pappadopoulos volunteered to return with her. The ship anchored six miles offshore on the morning of September 7, and he came ashore by launch to start his picture coverage at about ten o'clock.

Two of the most noteworthy characteristics of the scene were, he realized, beyond the reach of photography. One was the startling silence; normally a noisy thoroughfare, where the racket of street traffic mingled with harbor sounds in an agreeably constant uproar, the waterfront road was now as quiet as a forest path; the crowing of a rooster—not Beelzebub—could be heard from the other side of the city, as though the ruins had been farmland. Another was the stench of the dead bodies; noticeable a mile offshore, this was so strong on land that it caused him to retch violently and repeatedly before he reached the point from which he wished to make his first picture. While making this shot, however—it was a panorama of the ruins from a vantage point on the Bluff—he realized that the defect in his movie camera, which he had been unable to remedy completely, was not one which would seriously impair his coverage. The camera remained jammed, but there was very little moving. Stills would do full justice to the subject.

After his panorama of the ruins, Pappadopoulos made other shots on the Bluff. One was of a house that had belonged to a well-to-do American, of which the main feature had been a magnificent collection of ceramics. In its ruins he found the bodies of the family and a dozen of their servants in a curious condition typical of thousands of the corpses of those who had died of carbon monoxide poisoning during the fire. The heat had been sufficient to burn off their clothes but not their skin or even their hair. They looked like life-sized nude statues made out of shiny black porcelain. Unlike the household's real china, of which some was still intact, the glazed corpses would crumble at a touch.

Much the most durable things in Yokohama were the massive steel safes in which business firms kept their records, cash, and other valuables. Battered and blackened but still structurally intact, many of these safes were buried in the ruins of the business district. Soldiers, sailors or police were doing their best to stand guard, but some looting—punishable by death under martial law—was going on nonetheless. Pappadopoulos reasoned that a photograph or two of such scavengers, even if relatively stationary, would relieve the monotony of his lifeless landscapes and interiors. He saw a crew of six looters trying to pry open a strongbox, and set up his camera.

Too engrossed to notice him at first, the looters went on with their work until he made preparations for departing. One of them then apparently realized what had been happening—and that the film in the camera might constitute evidence that could lead to a death sentence. The six looters dropped the safe and made for Pappadopoulos. Now the agility developed at tennis served him to good advantage. After a scrambling chase through the ruins, he outdistanced his pursuers. When they returned to their treasure, he sat down to rest on a convenient bank—which proved to be a pile of corpses concealed under a deep drift of ashes.

Three days of diligent photography followed. During this time, Pappadopoulos lodged in a shanty made out of scraps of his own ruined house. A Lloyd's insurance inspector from Shanghai, who had been a fellow passenger on the *West O'Rowa*, shared his quarters. Neither had much to eat; Pappadopoulos had brought a bottle of whiskey off the ship, he found raw vegetables in his own and nearby gardens, and he got an egg or two from his former cook, who

turned up during his stay to guard the property. On his third afternoon, desperately hungry, Pappadopoulos made his way to the
waterfront where a United States Navy sentry told him that one
of the ships anchored offshore might be able to give him emergency
rations. Pappadopoulos left his camera and film with the sentry and
boarded a launch which took him to the *West O'Rowa*.

When he boarded the *West O'Rowa*, the first thing he discovered
was that she was already getting up steam for the journey back.
The second was that, because of confusion about his status in the
ship's company, he had been listed as a deserter from a relief party.
Before he could get the second matter straightened out, Pappadopoulos found himself in the brig. By the time he reached the captain
and explained his position, the ship was weighing anchor. The
captain was apologetic, but Pappadopoulos was nonetheless left to
choose between the alternatives of losing his pictures or of returning
to Yokohama with the launch that had brought him out and
awaiting a later passage to Kobe. He chose the latter and went back
to shore with a box of canned foodstuffs.

Having retrieved his camera and film from the sentry, Pappadopoulos began looking for another ship scheduled to depart for
Kobe. That afternoon he found one. She was the *Selma City*,
which had docked the day before the earthquake with a cargo
listed as cement. Unfortunately, when her officers tried to use
some of the cargo in patching a hole smashed through her plates
in one of the numerous harbor collisions, the cement proved
to be powdered milk that had been mislabeled to avoid import
duties. The powdered milk—just what Yokohama needed at the
moment—was speedily unloaded duty-free, but there was nothing
much that could be done about the damage to the *Selma City*.
Because of the hole in her side, she made slow going to Kobe—
three days and a half for a voyage which, Pappadopoulos learned
on his arrival, the *West O'Rowa* had made in less than two.

In Kobe, he learned that, by not sailing on the *West O'Rowa*, he had missed the market for his pictures. A newsreel editor had just bought coverage of the disaster in Tokyo and dispatched it to the United States. Pappadopoulos sold his films to a newspaper for five hundred dollars, which was far less than he had hoped to get for them. The same day, however, he had a stroke of luck—an assignment from a San Francisco brick company to do a complete film survey of the whole earthquake area at two hundred and fifty dollars a day. This job took two weeks and provided him with the money he needed to make a fresh start.

One purpose of this survey was to establish the comparative earthquake-resistant properties of brick, concrete, and ferroconcrete. In the course of it, Pappadopoulos examined the Imperial Hotel, aided by Mr. Inumaru, and reached the conclusion that the damage there had been 8 per cent, on a scale according to which 100 per cent would represent total destruction.

CHAPTER IX

MUSUBI

THE TYING TOGETHER

KIKUGORO ONOE I, who lived from 1717 to 1783, first in Kyoto and later in Edo, was the founder of a famous dynasty of actors in Japan's Kabuki Theater. Kikugoro Onoe VI, born in 1885, was a worthy heir to the tradition. His dancing in plays like *Chushingura*, or *Loyalty*, telling the classic story of the Forty-seven Ronin, was considered by the best critics to be unsurpassable. On September 1, Kikugoro VI was in Kamakura, staying near the house where his then mistress and later second wife, Chiyo Terajima, lived with her mother. Chiyo was one of the most renowned of Tokyo's geisha—outstanding both for her beauty and for her talent as a singer.

At Kamakura, Chiyo and Kikugoro caught a train for Tokyo at a few minutes before eleven o'clock—after a series of minor delays that almost made them miss it—and came into town together. Over the protests of her escort, who said that it was quite superfluous, Chiyo ran out onto the platform at Yokohama to send a telegram to her mother, letting her know that they had caught the train. As things turned out, the telegram saved the old lady's life; she had

168

just stepped out of her house to accept it from the delivery boy when the earthquake began and the house collapsed. By this time, Kikugoro and Chiyo had arrived in Tokyo and separated for the afternoon—she to go to her own house and he to the Ichimura Theater to rehearse for the opening presentation of the season two days later.

In addition to being a national celebrity—so well known that he was often referred to simply by his numerical nickname, The Sixth —Kikugoro was a confirmed fire buff and one who, like New York's late Mayor LaGuardia, was rarely averse to using the prerogatives of his position in the pursuit of his hobby. When the quake struck, just as the rehearsal was about to start, he realized that it meant not only the cancellation of his afternoon's work but also, in all probability, a rare chance for him to be a star spectator at a unique performance of the kind of drama which he most enjoyed. Even the role of witness naturally required the right costume and props. The Sixth sent a stagehand scampering off to the nearest fire station, where he was well known to all, to borrow a fireman's uniform. Arrayed in this, he set off in his car to lay in some supplies that would enable him to savor the coming spectacle without, so to speak, leaving his seat.

From an almost equally celebrated fellow actor named Baiko Onoe, Kikugoro borrowed a joint of meat, some eggs and a sack of rice; realizing that the electricity would be shut off, he also foresightedly laid in a stock of candles. Then, before proceeding to his own house in the suburb of Shiba, he stopped at Chiyo's to tell her to pack up her belongings and be ready to leave at a moment's notice. On reaching home, he sent a rickshaw to fetch her; and while awaiting her arrival, he put up a small marquee in his garden.

All these sophisticated preparations bore fruit in due course. That evening—when the Ichimura Theater burned down and also most of the Asakusa district, where Chiyo's house had been—they were able to watch the greatest conflagration in history from what amounted to box seats. Once or twice the flames came a bit too close for comfort, but there was never any real danger, and one of these moments actually provided the high point of the whole performance. When one of the storehouses behind the house caught fire from a spark in the wind, the great actor, still in his fireman's costume, ran to a nearby Buddhist temple where he borrowed a copious supply of the wooden flowerpots kept there for use in funeral ceremonies. Filling these with water pumped from his own well, he deftly extinguished the small blaze himself.

Neighbors who dropped in during the evening, some of them armed with old swords or bamboo spears, brought rumors that atrocities were being committed by the Koreans. The Sixth had long since graduated from the ranks of spear carriers, but he realized that the situation was the cue for action of some sort on his part. He went to the nearby headquarters of the Kempeitai, or military police, to seek direction. A helpful captain named Masahiko Amakasu, eager to please such an important artistic personage, not only provided expert advice but came back to the house with him, to make sure that he would not be molested. Amakasu, himself a theatrical buff, proved to be a congenial guest; he returned every evening during the anxious fortnight that followed. On the evening of the sixteenth, however, he left early, saying that he had important business to attend to and did not know when, or even whether, he would be able to return.

From The Sixth's house, Captain Amakasu went straight to Kempeitai headquarters and there attended to his business, which was important enough to make national headlines a few days later when there were again headlines to be made. The business consisted of entering the jail-cell of a prisoner named Sakae Osugi, locking an arm around his neck from behind, forcing him to the floor, planting a knee on his back and then giving his head a sharp jerk upward. When Sakae Osugi was dead—soundlessly and without bloodshed—the captain entered the next cell, occupied by Osugi's

wife, and disposed of her in much the same way. Perhaps he had
been excited by the first murder, for he was now a bit less adroit; her
efforts to cry for help aroused the occupant of a third cell. This
was the deceased couple's seven-year-old nephew, who had been
arrested under the mistaken impression that he was Osugi's son. To
silence his screams, the captain felt obliged to put an end to the
little boy also, using both hands around his scrawny throat.

Some of the background of the murders came to light a few days
later, at the prompt trial of Captain Amakasu. It developed that,
during the afternoon following the earthquake, Osugi, well-known
as a rabble-rouser and reputed anarchist, had been observed by
witnesses addressing segments of the crowd at the Imperial Palace
Plaza. According to these witnesses, he had seized the opportunity provided by a captive audience to make several revolutionary
speeches, reiterating the somewhat incongruous theme-phrase, "Remember Russia and never lay down your arms!" In the days after the
earthquake, when the police busied themselves in rounding up
known leftists and troublemakers, they had somehow missed Osugi.
Amakasu, in glancing through lists of persons arrested, had noted
the omission. On the fifteenth, he had personally rectified it by
ordering that Osugi be apprehended and brought in to his station.

Kikugoro VI's first knowledge about the "important business"
which had claimed the attention of his new-found crony came
when he read about it in the papers a few days later. What made
it especially shocking to him, as a sort of sinister *musubi*, or tying
together of loose ends, was that he was well acquainted with both
principals in the drama. Sakae Osugi had been his classmate in
grammar school; the actor remembered him as an exceptionally
bright boy and very likable. Coming from a poor family, he
regularly brought a lunch box which contained, instead of plain
rice like those of the others, a sort of hash made out of leftover
bean curds. Kikugoro, who rarely encountered such plebeian fare,

regarded these as a great delicacy and, already a precocious gourmet, he lost no chance to get a taste of them. Shared lunches had led to a close friendship, terminated when the two left school.

As to the actor's friendship with Captain Amakasu, this was also terminated, as suddenly as it had begun, by the latter's trial, which resulted in a ten-year prison sentence later substantially reduced. The two met again only once, many years later, by which time Amakasu himself was in the business end of the entertainment industry, as manager of the Manchuria Moving Picture Company. Kikugoro VI had been invited to dance at the coronation ceremonies of the puppet Emperor Pu-Yi of Manchukuo in 1934. On arriving in Dairen, he was astonished to find Amakasu waiting to welcome him on the station platform.

CONSIDERED IN THEIR CHRONOLOGICAL CONTEXT, both the murder of the alleged anarchist Osugi by Kempeitai Captain Amakasu and the outcome of the latter's trial may have been clues to the character of the period. Like the resilient, even exuberant, spirit with which the ruined cities had faced the huge task of reconstruction, they were perhaps evidence of the need to read some sort of meaning into the earthquake. The attempt to equate it with political upheaval, to which its consequences in physical destruction and social chaos bore superficial resemblance, was no doubt natural enough. Nonetheless it may also suggest that the conflict between rebellion and reaction, endemic in all human society, attains special intensity beneath the ceremonious surface of society in Japan.

As the work of reconstruction progressed, and as it became clear that in it the social pyramid was being rebuilt in much the same shape as before, other signs of stress and anxiety marred the blithe courage with which the capital had at first confronted the future. Some of these symptoms were short-lived and superficial—for example, certain morbidly slanderous stories in Tokyo newspapers, when they resumed publication, of imagined happenings after the earthquake in the harbor at Yokohama. As ill-founded as the earlier word-of-mouth rumors about the Koreans, these stories dealt with atrocities alleged to have been committed on board foreign liners; having followed the Western convention of rescuing women and children first, their officers were accused of taking the women out to sea, misusing them in various ways, and then tossing them overboard. Such fabrications gained little credence against the irrefutable evidence of Western good will in the form of relief efforts through the earthquake area. Other later indications of social malaise were more significant.

Under Home Minister Goto, as advised by Charles Beard, grand-scale reconstruction had naturally involved grand-scale research and committee work. In addition to the Relief Bureau, with its seven hundred workers, Home Minister Goto formed a Reconstruction Committee, with several hundred more. The plans devised by this group involved not merely the rebuilding of Tokyo, with wide streets and ferroconcrete apartment-and-office buildings clustered in occupationally segregated districts, but even major improvements on the harbor which alone were to cost 350 million yen.

As things developed, the harbor improvement soon began to seem superfluous, and the relocation of occupational groups in the population presently proved equally impractical. Most of the citizens of Tokyo had originally had good reasons for choosing the locations they had occupied before the fire. Now, for the same reasons, they wanted to stay in the same locations—just as the government itself wanted to stay in Tokyo—and Utopian proposals for moving had no appeal whatsoever. The reconstruction program, combined with the departure from the capital of hundreds of thousands of homeless workers to find refuge with country relatives, resulted in a serious labor shortage which made even modest rebuilding projects hard to execute. The result was that, while the Reconstruction Committee discussed long-range schemes for a new capital of unparalleled magnificence, Tokyo was being rebuilt overnight in an even more helter-skelter style than before, as a vast conglomeration of pine-board shacks with tin roofs and packing-case partitions.

Eventually the predicament of the Reconstruction Committee grew serious enough to warrant a special session of the Diet, which was convened on December 10. As a result of its deliberations, the government's share of the reconstruction budget was reduced from a billion and a half yen first to seven hundred and fifty million, then to six hundred million and finally to a little less than half a billion. Even this expression of mistrust, however, had less effect upon the Cabinet than an indirect consequence of the special session which took place on December 27. This was an attempted assassination of the Prince Regent, while on his way to open the session, by a deranged youth who apparently blamed him because a new social order had failed to grow out of the earthquake ruins.

Assassinations and attempted assassinations of important public personages occur often enough in Japan to be surrounded by their own special etiquette. Attempts on the life of the royal family, however, are something quite outside the normal run. This one resulted in the resignation of the entire cabinet and there were even some who felt that Home Minister Goto—upon whom responsibility for maintaining law and order rested most specifically— might feel impelled to draw his seppuku sword for ceremonial self-dispatch. The Viscount saw things differently, however, and apparently endorsed the attitude of the chief of the Tokyo Police Force, a young man named Matsutaro Shoriki, who assumed the brunt of the blame and resigned at the same time. Not long afterward, Shoriki, with Viscount Goto's financial assistance, entered upon a new and, as it proved, highly successful new career by buying a small newspaper called the *Yomiuri Shimbun*.

Comparable with the deterioration in domestic morale was a change for the worse in Japan's relations with the U.S. which,

though it derived more directly from certain subsequent developments in U.S. politics than from the earthquake, also had some connection with the latter. In 1924, motives of expediency caused the
U.S. to stop offering that haven to the poor and oppressed so movingly described on the base of the Statue of Liberty in favor of
limiting immigration from all countries to 150,000 a year. In effect-
ing this, each country was to be granted a "quota" based on the
number of its nationals already inside the U.S. Had this formula
been impartially applied, Japan's annual allowance would have
been the undeniably modest one of 146. The good character of these
immigrants, moreover, would have been guaranteed by an eminently
satisfactory arrangement set up by Theodore Roosevelt in 1907 and
known—somewhat euphemistically, it proved—as the "Gentleman's
Agreement." Instead of applying the formula devised for other countries, however, the new act included a special provision whereby the
Gentleman's Agreement would be unilaterally canceled and "Asi-
atics"—i.e., Japanese, since Chinese were already ruled out by a previous law—would be excluded altogether.

As a display of racial prejudice in its ugliest form, this provision of
the new bill aroused appropriate opposition, lead by Secretary of
State Hughes. Thinking to discourage its passage by the Senate, he
advised Japan's Ambassador Masakao Hanihara that it might be
helpful if the Ambassador wrote him a friendly personal letter
commenting on the effect that the passage of the bill might have in
Japan. This the Ambassador courteously did, pointing out, mildly
enough, that the bill stigmatized his compatriots as "unworthy and
undesirable" and that it could scarcely fail to have "serious consequences" in Japan.

At this point, Senator Henry Cabot Lodge of Massachusetts,
whose last major contribution to world progress had been to keep
the U.S. out of the League of Nations, perceived a good chance
to make another one. In the Senate debate, he intimated that Ambassador Hanihara's letter—which he was fully aware had been

written at the suggestion of Hughes—represented spontaneous "interference" in the internal affairs of the United States and that the phrase "serious consequences" amounted to an insolent threat of war. Aided by this adroit forensic gambit, the bill was duly enacted into law.

Whatever lay behind Japan's protracted self-exclusion from the rest of the world during the Tokugawa Shogunate, one point about it seems reasonably clear. This is that a Japanese aversion for foreigners which had lasted for two and a half centuries could scarcely have been expected to vanish overnight when Perry "opened up" Japan in 1853. Remnants of that aversion had, indeed, been suggested by many unhappy incidents during the early years of the Meiji restoration. If Japan's distrust of other nations had been to some extent dispelled by their sympathetic behavior immediately after the earthquake, this distrust was now revived and intensified. To Japan, the "Exclusion Act" seemed to be—as indeed it was, as far as its proponents were concerned—an expression of crude malice. As such, it did more than cancel all the good will toward the United States generated by the earthquake relief. It made the relief appear in retrospect to have been a deliberately hypocritical gesture.

In the mood of angry disillusionment thus created, Japan's militarists were able to launch the policy that, beginning with the Manchurian Incident, later led to the alliance with Hitler and eventually to Pearl Harbor. Thus, in one sense, both Lodge and Hanihara were right. The "Exclusion Act" did indeed have serious consequences; and the price which the United States eventually paid to prevent the yearly addition to its population of one hundred and forty-six carefully selected Japanese—who, if they had measured up to the standard of their predecessors, would all have been model citizens— was the Pacific War.

In the winter of 1924, all these gloomy developments lay far in the future. In Tokyo, Yokohama, and the other cities of the Kanto

Plain, reconstruction gathered impetus again under a new cabinet headed by Keigo Kiyoura. By 1929, most of the damage done by the quake had been restored; and, if the results were not quite those that had been originally envisaged by Goto and Beard, they were at least in some respects an improvement upon what had existed before the disaster.

Viscount Goto's most noteworthy contribution, which took the predictably appropriate form of an organization for research, was the Tokyo Seismological Institute. Backed, like the Tokyo Institute for Municipal Research, by the Yasuda family—whose philan-thropic interests expanded widely and rapidly after the catastrophe —this is the only organization of its kind in the world and the one most largely responsible for the vast increase in knowledge about earthquakes which has taken place since 1923. The Institute is presently headed by that worthy successor to Professors Omori and Imamaru in Japan's seismological hierarchy, Professor Chuji Tsuboi of Tokyo University.

In Tokyo, as in Yokohama, the municipal park system was en-larged to some extent as a result of the disaster. One enlargement took place when the heirs of Yoshio Yasuda presented the city with the Sumida River residence to which Dr. Ikeguchi and his family had repaired on the afternoon of September 1. Another occurred when the northernmost corner of the former Clothing De-pot—of which the remainder was later used for ordinary commercial purposes—was converted into an Earthquake Memorial Park. This park is dedicated to the memory of all those who died in the great earthquake-fire—and, since the Second World War, also to those who died in the great air-raid fire of March, 1945.

To the right of the main entrance of the Earthquake Memo-rial Park stands a small museum in which are to be found all sorts of odd mementos relating to the disaster. There one can see the sheet of corrugated iron that wrapped itself around the tree limb in the Yasuda garden, along with the limb itself, still entwined in the rusty metal. The battered bicycle frame found in another treetop, a wheel of the horse cart blown into the Yasuda pond, and numerous charts indicating the hour-by-hour progress of the fire and the location of major whirlwinds are also on display. For those curious about the earthquake's impact upon the minds of the young, the walls afford an exhibition of freehand drawings made long ago by earthquake foundlings in the art class of their special school. The museum is open on only a few days in every year and, nowadays, not many people visit it even on such days. It is not listed among the national attractions recommended by the Japan Travel Bureau, which professes to know what tourists like and makes sure that few escape without being exposed to the famous antiquities on view at Nikko, Nara, and Kyoto.

At the center of the Earthquake Memorial Park stands a temple of impressive size but not of any particular architectural distinction. This contains the ashes of all those cremated under gasoline at the Depot and by pine-log fire elsewhere in Tokyo. Its main hall is embellished by rather unsatisfactory oil paintings of memorable incidents in the disaster, such as the crash of the Twelve-Story Tower, the train wreck at Nebukawa and, of course, the holocaust at the Depot itself. Like the museum, this temple is rarely open to the general public, but on behalf of relatives who perished, it is visited quite regularly by many middle-aged or elderly people who were themselves survivors of the disaster in 1923. Much as the Clothing Depot did in the old days, the Earthquake Memorial Park serves as a playground and practice field for the children of the neighborhood. The scene is perhaps remarkable less as a reminder of the catastrophe than as evidence of how completely and how rapidly its scars have healed.

In this respect, the Great Kanto Earthquake provides an interesting contrast with what is doubtless its closest equivalent in Western history, the Lisbon Earthquake of All Saints' Day, 1755. This event, often regarded as marking the thunderous dawn of

the "Era of Enlightenment," had profound and lasting consequences for European culture in general and European literature in
particular. It dealt a death blow to the philosophy of Leibnitz, in-
spired Voltaire to the composition of *Candide* and enhanced the
fame and influence of Jean Jacques Rousseau, thus helping to
lay the foundation for the French Revolution and much of the
world's history since then. Its literary repercussions were still re-
verberating on its bicentennial which was commemorated by
T. D. Kendrick's completion of his small but valuable book *The
Lisbon Earthquake* in which he draws attention to the poem
that celebrated its centennial. This was "The Deacon's Masterpiece,
or the Wonderful One-Hoss Shay" by Oliver Wendell Holmes,
since

> It was on the terrible Earthquake-day
> That the Deacon finished the one-hoss shay.

The shattering impact of the Lisbon earthquake upon the consciousness of the Western world was, of course, due largely to the
fact that it took place not merely on All Saints' Day but also
at 9:30 A.M. when most of the devout were at Mass—and thus exposed to maximum danger of destruction. In an era when, much
more than is the case nowadays, the Almighty was held directly
responsible for the minute trivia of human existence, this dramatic
coincidence posed a grave dilemma: either God was capable of
astonishing carelessness or else he was thoroughly displeased with
the Portuguese, especially those resident in their capital. In the latter case, the question that arose was: Why? Voltaire framed it el-
oquently in a poem which served as a sort of curtain raiser to his
even more celebrated prose work:

> *Lisbonne, qui n'est plus, eût-elle plus de vices*
> *Que Londres, que Paris, plongés dans les délices?*
> *Lisbonne est abîmée, et l'on danse à Paris.*

In view of the peculiar circumstances, comparing the cultural consequences of the Lisbon catastrophe with those of its Tokyo successor may not be altogether fair. However, even in the case of the San Francisco disaster of 1906, which took place long after the start of the scientific age which its predecessor had helped to inaugurate, somewhat the same sort of contrast is discernible. Although picayune in comparison with those of its successor, the practical consequences of the San Francisco disaster have been recorded through two generations of American literature, journalism, art and related activities, ranging from a 1935 movie starring Nelson Eddy and Jeanette MacDonald to William Bronson's 1959 book, *The Earth Shook, the Sky Burned.*

Cultural aftershocks of the Great Kanto Earthquake have been as much smaller than those of its predecessors as its practical consequences were greater. So far as the author of the present volume has been able to determine, there are only two earlier books about it in English. One of these is *The Japanese Earthquake of 1923* by Charles Davison, which amounts to a sort of expanded codicil to his highly informative seismological textbook, *Major Earthquakes of the World.* The other is *The Great Earthquake of 1923 in Japan,* issued by the Bureau of Social Affairs of the Japan Home Office, upon which Davison's work is partly based and which is essentially a translated summary of social and seismological statistics. There are, of course, many substantial volumes about the Kanto Dai-shinsai in Japanese but practically all of these deal with it from the scientific point of view. So far as poetry, fiction, painting and allied arts in Japan are concerned, the most terrible catastrophe in history might just as well never have occurred at all.

For the spectacular reticence of the Japanese in regard to such a stupendous occurrence, various explanations might be advanced. Of these, perhaps the most plausible is that, for the past century, Japanese writers and artists have been so busy emulating their Western colleagues—just as their predecessors emulated the Chinese—that they have had little inclination to draw upon domestic sources of inspiration. However, it is equally true that earlier and only slightly less dreadful disasters were likewise largely ignored by Japan's otherwise inclusive art and literature, as proved by the exception to the rule represented by Hokusai's famous "Wave," which was no doubt a tsunami. Reticence about the Kanto Dai-shinsai may thus be paradoxically rooted in the same Japanese stoic tradition that expressed itself in the laconic phrase, Edo no Hana. In any case, outside the seismological libraries, the literature of the Kanto Dai-shinsai in the land of its occurrence is confined mainly to the newspaper files for the autumn of 1923; and these, for reasons previously mentioned, are notably far from complete.

The fragmentary character of the existing records of the event had certain specialized consequences in the composition of the present volume. Even today, few of the survivors of the earthquake have any very clear idea of what happened during it outside the particular areas with which they themselves were concerned. Trying to recreate any sort of general picture of the calamity resembled covering a news event rather than one which belongs to the category of history and involved much the same research procedures, based upon personal interviews. Since survivors who were old enough to remember what happened are now growing rapidly scarcer, the attempt seemed fairly justifiable. However, this is certainly not the place in which to try to thank the many informants who were kind enough to assist in the enterprise. What may be permissible in conclusion is a brief attempt to satisfy whatever curiosity may have been aroused about those whose experiences are described herein so much less movingly than they were communicated to the author. (For no one who lived through the Great Kanto Earthquake has forgotten what he or she was doing when it occurred and for a considerable, though varying, span of time thereafter; and the total recall of the participants in the events of that now distant September 1 produced a special sort of eloquence which no transcription can hope to recapture.)

IN MANY RESPECTS the most eloquent of the reminiscences which I had the privilege of hearing were those of Antonios Pappadopoulos, now the Honorary Greek Consul General in Yokohama. Listening to Mr. Pappadopoulos was inevitably a little like listening to a modernized and magnified first-person version of *The Odyssey*. The narrator shared with the hero of that mighty work both the knack of encountering crisis and the perhaps corollary capacity for coping with it. His easy familiarity with emergencies, well developed by the time of the earthquake and further perfected since, enable him to discuss the event with a detachment unique among those whom I questioned on the subject. However, his subsequent career has been so far from anticlimactic that it would be impractical here to summarize its high points, except as they relate to the catastrophe.

During the winter after the earthquake, Mr. Pappadopoulos re-established himself in Kobe as the part proprietor of an import agency for automotive machinery. His eventual partner in this venture was Major Morris Chichester-Smith, whose equally crisis-prone temperament made for commercial congeniality. Major Chichester-Smith later returned to England where he became a pillar of the Royal Aero Club while his partner stayed on in Japan until World War II, in which he and his older son enlisted in the Australian Army. After the war, Mrs. Pappadopoulos and their two sons remained in Australia while her husband stayed in Japan. In Yokohama, he now shares with Dante Dentici a bachelor establishment not far from the cliff over which bluff dwellers were hurling themselves when the latter heard their screams on the night after the earthquake.

For a full account of the lifelong adventures of Pappadopoulos the proper vehicle would, of course, have been an epic by Nikos Kazantzakis, whose modern sequel to *The Odyssey* is the major Greek classic of the current century. Such a volume was in immediate prospect a few years ago when Kazantzakis, paying a visit to Japan, naturally encountered Mr. Pappadopoulos without much delay. During a discussion of Russia, Kazantzakis asked him what he thought of Karl Marx, whereupon Pappadopoulos amiably replied that his feelings about Marx were identical with those of the Devil about holy water. Kazantzakis was charmed by this blithe approach, and the acquaintance between the two ripened rapidly. The great writer suggested that Pappadopoulos visit him in Greece, and the latter was preparing at last to return to his native land under these gala circumstances when, in 1957, Kazantzakis died, thus creating a crisis beyond the control of even his prospective visitor.

The 8-per cent earthquake damage inflicted upon the Imperial Hotel according to the Pappadopoulos survey was considerably exceeded by bombs dropped during World War II. The hotel, however, was repaired immediately afterward and still well-patronized during the autumn of 1960, when I lived there while gathering the material for this book. Wright's building, now known as "the old wing," is considerably exceeded in size by the new one, standing on the site of the pre-Wright "annex." New methods of earthquake-resistant construction have now made it possible to raise buildings so much higher in Tokyo that the capital now boasts a tower which exceeds both the Eiffel in Paris in height and its old twelve-story predecessor in Tokyo as a tourist attraction. The main purpose of this spectacular edifice is to broadcast the programs of Japan's booming TV industry, dominated by Matsutaro Shoriki, whose *Yomiuri Shimbun* has long been one of Tokyo's major dailies.

The old three-story Imperial is now again, as it was when first completed, economically unrealistic. No doubt it will presently be pulled down for something bigger and more compact, but during Wright's lifetime, characteristic Japanese consideration for its designer's feelings contributed to the decision of the directors to let it stand a while longer. Meanwhile, manager Inumaru, almost as unchanged in appearance as he is in vitality, runs the establishment as energetically as ever, when not indulging his long-established habit of global circumnavigation.

The aged Baron Okura, whom Inumaru found on the lawn of his villa the morning after the earthquake, lived only long enough to recoup his fortune, but his son Kihichiro, who discarded his hereditary title in common with the rest of Japan's peerage after World War II, retained his inherited longevity. Less concerned with the Imperial than his father, he is even more enthusiastically addicted to the hotel business in general and is presently engaged in rearing a huge one of his own, to be completed in ample time for Tokyo's 1964 Olympic Games. The site of this establishment is the property which once housed his father's villa and museum, on the high ground adjoining the boundary of the American Embassy once transgressed by the secret subterranean passage. One frequent visitor to the Embassy, during his recent term as president of Tokyo's American Chamber of Commerce, was Mr. Howard Van Zandt, whose father had had the foresight to leave Yokohama for Chicago during the summer of 1923.

The present tenant of the Embassy Residence is Edwin Old-father Reischauer, son of the founder of Tokyo's Aural School for the Deaf and of the Dr. August Reischauer who mistook the earthquake-fire for a new volcano when he saw it by night from Karuizawa. A boy of twelve at the time of the catastrophe, Edwin O. Reischauer grew up to become a professor like his father and America's foremost authority on Japanese history. His wife is the former Haruko Matsukata, granddaughter of the old Prince and the niece of Saburo who retired a few years ago as head of the Domei Press.

The former Makiko Aoki, now Mrs. Makiko Iida, teaches in a secondary school some miles from the Honjo area where, however, she still lives, not far from the spectacle-frame shop which is still in business on its old site. The family disposed of its interest in the factory some years ago, but the store is still run by Makiko's younger brother, the one who was blown away from her at the Clothing Depot during the tornado. Their father's death occurred during a period when Makiko was living in Manchuria with her late husband. Her neighbors there included not only Captain Masahiko (meaning The Righteous One) Amakasu but also a more important moving-picture executive named Nagamasa Kawakita. Kawakita—the schoolboy who had been told by the hospital telegraph clerk that Japan no longer existed—now heads one of Tokyo's biggest producing companies.

One of the few days when the Earthquake Memorial Temple is open to the public is September 1, when a commemorative ceremony is held there. These ceremonies usually attract a considerable number of those who have special reason to recall the catastrophe, and it was after one of them that I was first introduced to Dr. Eikichi Ikeguchi. Having already been told something about his experiences in the fire, I felt reluctant to bring up the subject until the doctor himself introduced it by saying that fewer people came to the ceremony now than in former years. When I said that I was gathering material for a book about the earthquake, the doctor suggested that I come to his house some afternoon when there would be more time to tell me about it. "If I get started talking, I may go on for a long time," he said. This made me suspect that, while he seldom had occasion to speak to anyone on the subject, it was never far from his thoughts, and also that he might welcome an opportunity to unburden his mind to a stranger who was also a foreigner.

Dr. Ikeguchi was a small slight man the exceptional pallor of whose face and hands might easily have been taken for a natural absence of skin pigmentation, if one had not known about the burns. When recalling the details of the earthquake, he spoke in a low monotone but so fast and steadily that the lady who was interpreting for me had difficulty in keeping up and found it a little hard to interrupt from time to time, so as to give me the gist of what he had been saying. We called on the doctor three times at his small house not more than five minutes' walk from the Memorial Park and the Yasuda residence garden. It was not until my third visit that he came to the part of his recollections which dealt with what happened after he had been taken by car to the house of his wife's family.

The car had had to stop some distance away from the house because of the condition of the road, and the driver, leaving the doctor behind, went on to tell the family of his arrival and to procure a stretcher. Waiting in the car, the doctor wondered why it took so long, but eventually he heard the voice of his brother-in-law who came to the car and explained the cause of the delay. The family had supposed that he was dead and, seeing him at a distance, had been unable to recognize him, owing to his disfigurement and to the condition of his clothes. Only now, hearing him speak and in doing so mention the names of the children, could they feel sure of his identity. They brought him into the house where they assured him that they had found the bodies of his wife and children and had attended to their burial.

"I cannot tell you how relieved I was when I learned that the bodies of my family had been taken care of," said Dr. Ikeguchi in telling the story.

Despite his relief, or because this meant that his mission was accomplished, the doctor had no further will to live and for some time refused to eat. Nonetheless, he went on living and, by July of the following year, though still in bandages, approached the end of his convalescence. When his hair began to grow again, he left Tokyo to visit hot springs in the west of Japan, as far away as possible, in hopes that they would help him.

"I must say," said Dr. Ikeguchi, "I visited practically every single hot spring in that area. I could not stay more than a day or two at any one place because by then I got used to it and could think of nothing but my memories of that day. Still, as the time went by, I became more resigned. I came to think that, after all, there should be someone to pay homage to the grave of my family. I then returned to my old place here and resumed my practice."

Several years after he resumed his practice, Dr. Ikeguchi married again. A dozen or so years after that, he and his second wife, who brought us tea while we talked, had a daughter who is now a girl of high-school age. During the Second World War, when the district burned again on the night of March 10, at the cost of 100,000 more lives, the Honjo district naturally had the worst conflagration. This time, however, there was no tornado, and from past experience the doctor knew which way the flames would go. He had no trouble in evading the fire.

Courage, we are told, is grace under pressure, and this may well be true. Perhaps, too, as the definition suggests, it is best exemplified for our era by a well-paid athlete in narrow trousers waving a cloth at some puzzled animal to the cheers of the grandstand. This seems to me more dubious, but that may not have much bearing on the matter. In any case, the Japanese, as is well known, have a custom of bowing when they say goodbye. I was glad to conform with this on taking leave of Dr. Ikeguchi.

ACKNOWLEDGMENTS

While assuming full responsibility for whatever errors of fact this book may contain, the author wishes to acknowledge here his deep obligation to all those who, either directly or through the printed word, provided the material upon which it is based.

Among the persons who contributed information either in the form of recollections of their experiences in the earthquake or in the form of knowledge of the circumstances involved, especial thanks are due to the following: Mr. Darrell Berrigan, Mr. Paul Blum, Mr. Robert Blum, Mr. Cooper Blyth, Mr. Don Brown, Mr. Lewis Bush, Dr. Perry Byerly, Miss Ruth Cox, Mr. Dante Dentici, Mr. Ray Downs, Mr. Motohiko Fuji-yama-Tanaka, Mr. J. E. Gregory, Mr. Tsutomo Goto, Mr. George Hel-yer, Mr. Ernest Hoberecht, Dr. Gunji Hosono, Mr. Frank Huggins, Mrs. Makiko Aoki Iida, Dr. Nobutaka Ike, Dr. Eikichi Ikeguchi, Mr. Tetsuzo Inumaru, Mr. Tsuneyuki Isono, Dr. Robert J. Lifton, Mr. David Mackensie, Mr. James Day Mason, Mr. Saburo Matsukata, Mr. Abbot L. Moffet, Mr. Ian Mutsu, Mr. Kuniharu Namikata, Mr. Yozo Nomura, former Baron Kihichiro Okura, Mr. Antonios Pappadopoulos, Mr. H. V. Redman, the Hon. Edwin O. Reischauer, Mr. Samuel Sobokin, Mr. and Mrs. James L. Stewart, Mr. Frederick C. Taylor, Mr. Moto Takata, Mr. Howard F. Van Zandt, Miss Florence Wells, Miss Jane Wilson, Mr. William P. Woodard, and Mr. John Yashiro.

Among books consulted for material bearing either on the earthquake itself or on the period in which it occurred, the author acknowledges especial indebtedness to the following:

Bronson, William Knox, *The Earth Shook, the Sky Burned*, Doubleday & Company, Inc., New York, 1959.

Bureau of Reconstruction, Home Office, Japan, compilers, *The Outline of the Reconstruction Work in Tokyo and Yokohama*, Tokyo, 1929.

Bureau of Social Affairs, Home Office, Japan, compilers, *The Great Earthquake of 1923 in Japan*, Tokyo, 1926.

Bush, Lewis William, *Land of the Dragonfly*, Robert Hale, Ltd., London, 1959.

Davison, Charles, *The Japanese Earthquake of 1923*, Thomas Masby & Co., London, 1931.

Drexler, Arthur, *The Architecture of Japan*, Museum of Modern Art, New York, 1955.

Griswold, Alfred Whitney, *The Far Eastern Policy of the United States*, Harcourt, Brace & Company, Inc., New York, 1938.

Harris, Townsend, *The Complete Journal of Townsend Harris*, Charles E. Tuttle Company, Tokyo and Rutland, Vt., 1959.

Imamura, Akitsune, *Theoretical and Applied Seismology*, Maruzen Co., Tokyo, 1937.

Japan Year Book Office, *The Japan Year Book*, 1924, Tokyo, 1924.

Kendrick, Sir Thomas Downing, *The Lisbon Earthquake*, J. B. Lippincott Company, Philadelphia, 1957.

Leet, Lewis Don, *Causes of Catastrophe: Earthquakes, Volcanoes, Tidal Waves, and Hurricanes*, Whittlesey House, McGraw-Hill Book Company, Inc., New York, 1948.

Milne, John, *Earthquakes and Other Earth Movements*, Kegan Paul, Trench, Trübner & Co. Ltd., London, 1903.

Mutsu, Countess Iso, *Kamakura, Fact and Legend*, Times Publishing Co., Ltd., Tokyo, 1930.

Richter, Charles Francis, *Elementary Seismology*, W. H. Freeman & Company, San Francisco, 1958.

Tokyo Municipal Office, *The Reconstruction of Tokyo*, Tokyo, 1933.

Transactions of the Asiatic Society of Japan, R. Meiklejohn & Co., Yokohama, 1886, vol. 14 et seq.

Williams, Harold Stannett, *Tales of Foreign Settlements in Japan*,

Charles E. Tuttle Company, Tokyo and Rutland, Vt., 1959.
Wolfenstein, Martha, *Disaster, a Psychological Essay,* Routledge & Kegan Paul, Ltd., London, 1957.
Young, Morgan, *Japan Under Taisho Tenno, 1912-1926,* George Allen & Unwin, Ltd., London, 1928.

Finally, and most particularly, the author expresses deep gratitude to Dr. Chuji Tsuboi of Tokyo University for his patient course of private instruction in the rudiments of seismology; to Mrs. Kazuko Okamura for her adroit and indefatigable assistance in research and translation; to Mr. Seiichi Fukuoka of the Japan office of the *Reader's Digest* for first suggesting the possibility of undertaking the book; and to Mr. Hobart Lewis, Executive Editor of the *Reader's Digest,* for his help and encouragement in carrying the undertaking to its final conclusion.

ABOUT THE AUTHOR

NOEL F. BUSCH *was born in New York City, grew up there and in Oyster Bay, Long Island, and attended St. George's School and Princeton University. He left the latter in 1927 to join the staff of* Time *magazine which had been founded four years previously by his cousin, the late Briton Hadden, and Henry R. Luce. After ten years on* Time, *he became a senior editor of the newly founded* Life, *for which he was later at various times article editor, war correspondent and staff writer. He left* Life *in 1952 to join the Asia Foundation, of which he was the representative in Japan from 1952 to 1954 and in Thailand from 1954 to 1958.*

Previous books by Noel F. Busch include My Unconsidered Judgment; What Manner of Man?, *a biography of FDR;* Fallen Sun, *a Report on Japan;* Briton Hadden, *a Biography;* Adlai E. Stevenson of Illinois, *a Portrait; and* Thailand, *an Introdu   n to* Modern Siam. *He has contributed to a wide range of maga   including* The New Yorker, *the* Saturday Evening Post, *the   ic   nd* Horizon, *and is at present a staff writer for* Reader's Di

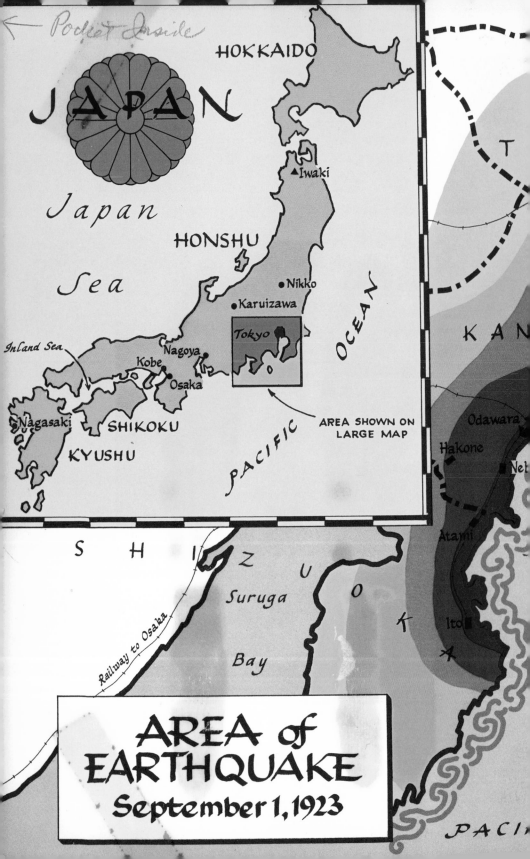

AREA of
EARTHQUAKE
September 1, 1923